# Shakespeare's Body Parts

# Shakespeare's Body Parts

*Figuring Sovereignty in the History Plays*

Huw Griffiths

EDINBURGH
University Press

Edinburgh University Press is one of the leading university presses in the UK. We publish academic books and journals in our selected subject areas across the humanities and social sciences, combining cutting-edge scholarship with high editorial and production values to produce academic works of lasting importance. For more information visit our website: edinburghuniversitypress.com

© Huw Griffiths, 2020, 2022

Edinburgh University Press Ltd
The Tun – Holyrood Road
12(2f) Jackson's Entry
Edinburgh EH8 8PJ

First published in hardback by Edinburgh University Press 2020

Typeset in 10.5/13 Adobe Sabon by
Servis Filmsetting Ltd, Stockport, Cheshire

A CIP record for this book is available from the British Library

ISBN 978 1 4744 4870 3 (hardback)
ISBN 978 1 4744 4871 0 (paperback)
ISBN 978 1 4744 4872 7 (webready PDF)
ISBN 978 1 4744 4873 4 (epub)

The right of Huw Griffiths to be identified as the author of this work has been asserted in accordance with the Copyright, Designs and Patents Act 1988, and the Copyright and Related Rights Regulations 2003 (SI No. 2498).

## Contents

| | |
|---|---|
| Preface | vii |
| Acknowledgements | xi |
| Introduction: The Baroque Body Parts of *Henry VI* Part Two | 1 |
| 1. Richard II as Robinson Crusoe: Sovereignty and the Impossibility of Solitude | 35 |
| 2. Necks, Throats and Windpipes in *Henry V*: Sovereignty Translated | 59 |
| 3. Prosthetic Hands in *King John* | 75 |
| 4. Copious Sovereignty in the *Henry IV* Plays | 101 |
| 5. 'My kingdom for a horse': Bestial Sovereignty in *Richard III* | 121 |
| Bibliography | 141 |
| Index | 147 |

# *Preface*

This book is avowedly formalist. I take the foremost metaphor of early modern political thought – the 'body politic' – and account for some aspects of just one of its many journeys: through the 1590s English history plays written by William Shakespeare. As my title suggests, in these texts this metaphor is most often encountered in refracted form: cut up and disarticulated. Two of the chapters focus on very particular body parts: hands in *King John*; necks and throats in *Henry V*. Other chapters discover more variously distributed bodies and body parts, all unyoked from the idea of a discrete, coherent and unified personhood that informs some other 'bodies politic' in the period. In particular, Shakespeare's body parts resist absolutist forms of sovereignty that would locate an inalienable political authority in the person of the king. Shakespeare's bodies are much too various for any such claims to be sustainable.

Why a formalist approach? Two reasons. One is that we understand politics through form. In so far as political systems and theories might be understood as the relationship of parts to wholes, these are always questions of form. The other is that Shakespeare is a very idiosyncratic kind of writer, one whose usual practice is to confute, confuse and multiply. During the sixteenth century, England and Wales and other European monarchical states witnessed a concentration of political authority within centralising monarchies and court bureaucracies. This is not, of course, the whole story of early modern political thought; there is also a well-documented tradition of republicanism, and of more corporate forms of governance. But Shakespeare's English histories are a series of plays that pay relentless attention to the apparently singular person of the king. They are unlike some history plays by Shakespeare's contemporaries which are often more likely to take in broader views of English society. For example, Heywood's two-part *Edward IV* plays concentrate just as much, if not more, on Jane Shore as on the king. And some plays either focus on figures other than the king, such as the multi-authored *Sir Thomas More*, or marginalise the king within much more diffuse narratives, such as Thomas Dekker's *The Shoemaker's Holiday*. By contrast, Shakespeare's histories, however much individually they occasionally stray away from their central figure, nevertheless return time and again to the lone figure of the king.

Each of these plays, however, reveals that singular, solitary figure to be multiple. For Shakespeare, sovereignty is best understood not as inalienable but as only ever inevitably alienated: contingent and on the move. And so, the corollary of this particular understanding is not a unified 'body politic', but a collection of body parts. David Hillman and Carlo Mazzio write that the early modern period is one in which, 'The negotiation between parts and wholes . . . became a specially vexed issue in the somatic structures of early modern Europe.'[1] That is, with the development of such things as anatomy theatres, or more atomised and conflicted conceptions of subjectivity, the idea of a unitary 'person' was not always to be taken for granted. In these plays, however much they take the king, himself, as their main subject matter, the person of the king is nevertheless revealed as always disjointed and fragmented.

One way of construing the formal properties of these plays would be through genre. It has been particularly difficult to place the generic parameters of the history plays. The most powerful account of the plays' investments in narrative patterns is Phyllis Rackin's *Stages of History*, in which she relates the inconsistencies of the plays' generic markers (sometimes tragic, sometimes seemingly more comic) to developments in early modern historiography.[2] On the one hand, there are providential narratives that see history working out through a pattern ordained by God, and the seeming providential tragedy of *Richard III* would seem to fit this pattern. On the other hand, there are histories that are more inspired by the contingencies of man-made history, particularly as being developed in early modern Italian historiography, associated with figures such as Machiavelli, in which events are related not to the will of God but to the judgements of people. The complexities of the *Henry IV* plays would seem most to fit this mode of historiographical thought. While I also see the history plays as caught between metaphysical imperatives and human contingencies, I relate this not to changes in historiographical thought but to a contention between absolutist conceptions of sovereignty and more distributed understandings of politics. For Shakespeare's history plays, these more distributed forms cannot, yet, be construed within Foucault's understanding of 'governmentality', the systematisation of the state and the totalising relocation of sovereignty within the bureaucracies of the modern state that he describes in his *Collège de France* lectures.³ Shakespeare's resistances to absolutism come, rather, in his peculiar forms of *poesis*, his imaginative reworking of the tropes of sovereignty. And so, rather than overarching generic form, I focus here on smaller examples of the plays' formal properties – their use of figures of speech such as *copia*, metonymy and metaphor, and the relationships that they imagine between dramatic speech and personhood.

In the Introduction, I begin with illustrations of some of Shakespeare's particular uses of body-based metaphors in the history plays. *Henry VI* part two provides good material for this because, between the original octavo publication and the folio text of the play, Shakespeare has substantially augmented the dialogue. And these additions almost entirely comprise a massive expansion in the variety of bodies and body parts that he refers to in the dialogue. I place this practice against the context of some recent critical work on the body: materialist approaches and work in the areas of political theory and 'political theology'. Chapter 1 further sets up the book with a focus on the impossible solitudes of Richard II in the play of that name. There follow two chapters that take particular body parts – necks and throats in *Henry V* and, then, hands in *King John* – as foci for the discussion of sovereignty and political responsibility. Despite the importance of capital punishment to the establishment of Henry V's power, the neck becomes a site wherein sovereign agency is in translation and in transition, posing questions about the legitimacy of the exceptionalist sovereignty upon which the act of capital punishment depends. *King John* asks questions about the extent to which a subject is obliged to act on behalf of, or as deputy for, a king claiming an absolute control, and it does this through the metonym of the hand. The two final chapters – one on the two *Henry IV* plays and one on *Richard III* – move away from individual body parts to consider more disseminated structures and forms. Shakespeare's customarily pervasive use of the rhetorical trope of *copia* reaches an extreme in the dialogue of the *Henry IV* plays. The vagrant bodies of these plays spin out and away from a sovereign centre that is represented as empty. Finally, *Richard III* is a play which directs our attention more than any other to the singular, exceptional person of the monarch, albeit an illegitimate one. In this play, Shakespeare gives us the dark empty heart of an early modern politics increasingly organised around the excepted person of the king.

## Notes

1. David Hillman and Carlo Mazzio, 'Introduction', in David Hillman and Carlo Mazzio (eds), *The Body in Parts: Fantasies of Corporeality in Early Modern Europe* (New York: Routledge, 1997), p. xiii.
2. Phyllis Rackin, *Stages of History: Shakespeare's English Chronicles* (Ithaca: Cornell University Press, 1990).
3. See Michel Foucault, *'Society Must Be Defended': Lectures at the Collège de France 1975–1976*, trans. David Macey (New York: Picador, 2003); and Michel Foucault, *The Birth of Biopolitics: Lectures at the Collège de France*, trans. Graham Burchill (London: Palgrave, 2008).

# *Acknowledgements*

Not unlike Richard II or, perhaps, a little bit more like Richard III, I have a fatal tendency to think of myself as self-sufficient. And, in truth, like a lot of academic work in the humanities, this book is the product of long periods of solitude. However, as with those two kings, this isolation is neither sustainable nor wholly accurate. I would particularly like to give a very belated and heartfelt thank you to my two PhD supervisors, Mike Bath and Alison Thorne. Alison gave me the opportunity to give my first ever Shakespeare lecture at the University of Strathclyde. It was on *Richard II*. And I have enjoyed thinking, talking and writing about Shakespeare's English history plays ever since.

I would like to thank colleagues past and present at the universities of Canterbury (New Zealand) and Sydney (Australia). The book was initially dreamt up, and then written, between the two institutions. Erin Mackie, Jed Mayer, Claire Hero, Nicola Parsons, Kate Lilley, Melissa Hardie, Peter Marks and Liam Semler have been exemplary colleagues, and have all contributed to the book in one way or another. Fellow participants in the University of Sydney's EMLAC (Early Modern Literature and Culture) seminar have been an important source of intellectual stimulus. Duncan Ivison kindly worked as a research mentor in the early stages of the project, seeing the production of the *King John* chapter, an earlier version of which appeared in *Exemplaria*. Other thanks go to Jonathan Gil Harris, for hosting a paper that I gave on some aspects of the book at George Washington University. Writing and giving that paper and, in the process, realising both the positive aspects and the shortcomings of my approach helped to generate the eventual direction of the project.

I would also like to acknowledge a debt of gratitude to the theatre director, Benedict Andrews, a debt that is invisible in the footnotes. He was kind enough to talk to me about his extraordinary eight-hour production of the entire cycle of the history plays, *The Wars of the Roses*, and also to let me in to watch rehearsals in 2009. Even though this book does not consider contemporary performance, his compelling account of the violent poetry of these plays has been something that I have returned to again and again in my thoughts.

And finally, thanks go to my family and my partner: to my parents, Diane and David Griffiths, for their always optimistic support, and to my partner, Angus Beadie, for his love and companionship, and for not caring that much about Shakespeare.

# Introduction: The Baroque Body Parts of *Henry VI* Part Two

The first English history play in which Shakespeare had a hand was published in 1594 as *The First Part of the Contention Betwixt the Two Famous Houses of Yorke and Lancaster*.[1] The text is based on an initial performance of the play from a few years earlier, around 1590–91, that had marked the start of a decade in which Shakespeare devoted much of his time to writing plays based on events surrounding the civil wars of the two preceding centuries. In a greatly expanded version, this play reappears as the *Second Part of Henry the Sixt* (*Henry VI* part two from now on) in the 1623 First Folio edition of Shakespeare's plays. The distinction between the two different printed texts is almost entirely one of length. The characters, the narrative, the sequencing of the scenes, even the specific order of the dialogue – these are all more or less exactly the same. Individual speeches are, however, often significantly longer in the folio text than they are in the 1594 octavo text. What is more, these newly drawn-out speeches are a particular feature of those parts of the play that recent editors have most confidently identified as the work of Shakespeare.[2] What makes the speeches longer is never any obvious change in their meaning or intent but, rather, a massive extension and proliferation of the metaphors that Shakespeare uses to describe and negotiate forms of authority.

These augmented and proliferating figurations might be seen as baroque, both in terms of their elaborate form and in their semantic drift away from any clear, organising principle, what Roland Greene calls the 'oversized utterances' and 'overdeveloped figuration' that can be seen as characteristic of the baroque.[3] Furthermore, the revisions always, throughout the play, consist of multiple references to body parts, and to bodies both human and animal. From these changes, in which sovereignty becomes increasingly figured through disarticulated body parts, we learn a lot about Shakespeare's approach to questions that permeated early modern political life and thought, and that occupy these plays.

A typical example of these expanded uses of metaphor falls in the earliest scene that current editors are most confident in assigning to Shakespeare. This is the scene in which Queen Margaret persuades her husband, King Henry VI, that Humphrey, Duke of Gloucester, is no longer to be trusted. It is a scene that bristles with conflicting and conflicted arguments over the limits and affordances of sovereign power. Queen Margaret goes about her work of undermining Gloucester in the eyes of the king, and describes the duke as becoming too proud and ambitious. In *The First Part of the Contention*, she makes her case with remarkable efficiency, using one central idea, or *topos*, to anchor her point: Duke Humphrey's increasing lack of sociability. In this earlier text this is given simply as reliable factual evidence of his ambition rather than, as later, the basis for metaphorical speculation:

> The time hath bene, but now that time has past,
> That none so humble as Duke Humphrey was:
> But now let one meete him even in the morne,
> When every one will give the time of day,
> And he will neither move nor speake to us.
> See you not how the Commons follow him
> In troupes, crying, God save the good Duke Humphrey,
> And with long life, Jesus preserve his grace,
> Honouring him as if he were their King.
> Gloster is no little man in England,
> And if he list to stir commotions,
> Tys likely that the people wil follow him.[4]

Margaret's clear point is that 'Gloster' is overstepping his role and being treated 'as if he were ... king'. This is just one in a long line of crises for Henry VI's authority in the three Henry VI plays, but Margaret's speech dwells on very specific actions and reactions – meeting/speaking/not speaking/following – that allow her to substantiate her point with appropriate evidence. Her links of symptom to cause are almost forensic in their clarity.

This same speech, in the folio version, is longer. Much longer. Where the speech in *The First Part of the Contention* describes specific actions, the folio text arrests that action at every step of the way. Metaphors pile up on top of each other, burying their referent out of sight. Where the speech in the earlier text deals primarily in specific, identifiable acts, the later text sees anything concrete fade into the background, supplanted by an elaborate carapace of metaphor, simile and metonymy. Sentences are stretched beyond their capacity, with successive clauses allowing room for more and more metaphorical and metonymic ideations of the relationships that Margaret seeks to describe:

> We know the time since he was mild and affable,
> And if we did but glance a far-off look
> Immediately he was upon his knee,
> That all the court admired him for his submission.
> But meet him now, and be it in the morn
> When everyone will give the time of day,
> He knits his brow, and shows an angry eye,
> And passeth by with stiff unbowèd knee,
> Disdaining duty that to us belongs.
> Small curs are not regarded when they grin,
> But great men tremble when the lion roars,
> And Humphrey is no little man in England.
> First note that he is near to you in descent,
> And should you fall, is the next will mount.
> Meseemeth that it is no policy,
> Respecting what a rancorous mind he bears
> And his advantage following your decease,
> That he should come about your royal person,
> Or be admitted to your highness' Council.
> By flattery hath he won the commons' hearts,
> And when he please to make commotïon,
> 'Tis to be feared they all will follow him.
> Now 'tis the spring, and weeds are shallow-rooted;
> Suffer them now, and they'll o'ergrow the garden,
> And choke the herbs for want of husbandry. (9.9–33)[5]

What *The First Part of the Contention* accomplishes in twelve lines now takes Queen Margaret twenty-five lines. In a change that is typical of the differences between these two versions of the play, the speech more than doubles in length. Shakespeare does introduce one new idea into the folio speech: a greater sense of danger that comes from Duke Humphrey's proximity to the throne, both physically ('admitted to your highness' Council') and in terms of heredity ('near to you in descent'). But Margaret's message is not fundamentally changed. Rather, the expansion is brought about by a substantial increase in the number and scope of the metaphors that Margaret uses to work through the problems of sovereign authority that are implied, if not elaborated, in the earlier version.

The distinction between the two speeches, I would say, is the difference between analogy and *poesis*, between described events as evidence for a particular crisis (albeit one of Margaret's own creation) and language that now takes on a life, or lives, of its own. At the start of the speech, folio Margaret does not just offer a brief comment on Humphrey's uncustomary surliness, but translates this observation into a symbolic blazon of a disobedient body: from a man who was previously 'immediately upon his knee' if the king and queen so much as glanced at him, to a man who now has a knitted brow, an angry eye and 'unbowèd knee'. The 'knee' is no longer merely incidental to the particular action of kneeling but is invested with more meaning by the queen, and it comes to work as a metonym not just for Humphrey's body but for what Margaret (wrongly) sees as his disloyalty. Throughout the history plays, in dialogue similar to this, Shakespeare focuses attention on particular body parts as locations in which sovereign authority is either formed or is broken apart. Knees, understandably, become a significant aspect of this interest in individual body parts. Both in this play and in *Richard II* – the two plays that are most concerned with the protocols of deference, and with a lack of proper deference to the crown at moments of crisis – knees feature very heavily. The 'Online Shakespeare Concordance' has these two plays, together with *Coriolanus*, as the top three in the 'knee' count. In Margaret's extended speech, however, the body parts are multiple and even the perfunctory statement of *The First Part of the Contention*, that 'the Commons follow him / In troupes', is augmented to include more body parts: 'By flattery hath he won the commons' hearts, / And when he please to make commotïon, / 'Tis to be feared they all will follow him'. The people are, in the extended version, represented through the metonymy of their hearts. The incursion of some animals – the 'small curs' and the roaring lion – into Margaret's phantasmagoria of rebellion and sovereign authority is also typical of the way that the language of the folio text gets extended. Potentially persuasive in isolation, together these different strands of metaphor and metonymy generate a more general impression that, in speaking about sovereignty, Shakespeare's characters often struggle to provide precise locations for their ideas. Ideas and similes, metaphors and metonymies all metastasise, contending with each other to supply an appropriate vehicle for the tenor of sovereign power which is, nevertheless, seemingly impossible to pin down. The referent for this language, no longer anchored by the evidentiary purposes of analogy, becomes increasingly hard to identify.

My identification of this metastasising language as 'baroque' is a purposeful choice. Not only is this description a way to connect the forms of Shakespeare's writing with the political forms of early modern sovereignty, it also helps me to introduce Walter Benjamin's account of the German seventeenth-century *Trauerspiel*, or 'martyr play', as a generative framework for understanding the work that is accomplished by Shakespeare's ever-increasing body parts in this, and other, of his history plays. Shakespeare's proliferating metaphors instantiate an aesthetic that turns away from classical strategies of representation, a turn that might be thought of as characteristic of the baroque, in the terms within which Benjamin discusses it in *The Origin of German Tragic*

*Drama*, a discussion taken up and continued by Gilles Deleuze in *The Fold*, and by Christopher Pye in *The Storm at Sea*. Benjamin describes an aesthetic mode in which a 'massive ornamental layer of truly baroque stucco conceals the keystone' and associates this with a dramatic form, the *Trauerspielen*, a kind of drama that, he argues, avoids eschatological or metaphysical explanations for the actions of its central monarchs.[6] The baroque, he writes, 'knows no eschatology; and, for that reason, does not advance any mechanism by which all earthly things are gathered in together and exalted before being consigned to their end'.[7] It is not so much that the 'keystone' is concealed as that it is absent, unnecessary even. If we are not overly concerned by periodisation – and both Benjamin and Deleuze invite us to consider a baroque aesthetic which, while emerging from specific historical circumstances, cannot be contained within a linear narrative of artistic development – then the multiple bodily forms in the language of the history plays can be read within the aesthetico-political domain of the baroque.[8] Deleuze describes 'fold after fold', as he stretches the baroque, by means of the figure of the fold, beyond its undeniable local origins in the early seventeenth century.[9] And, as Philip Lorenz writes, Benjamin's interest in the baroque is primarily determined by the ways in which he recognises the concerns of modernity in the crises of sovereignty that develop throughout the early modern period, in coincidence with the baroque. These shared concerns include, Lorenz writes, 'the virtualisation of politics'.[10] As Shakespeare shifts his language away from the evidentiary work of analogy to the generative work of *poesis*, there is a sense in which the political relationships within the history plays are rendered more 'virtual' or, at least, more potentially alienable from any founding idea of what constitutes sovereign power.

There is an unstoppable generation of bodies and bodily metaphors in the history plays; Shakespeare folds image into image, unable or unwilling to resolve them into a coherent representation of sovereignty. By means of the endlessly proliferating fold, the production of ornament and detail unanchored by a secure semantic schema, the baroque, as Deleuze continues to pronounce, 'invents the infinite work or process'.[11] And, for Shakespeare's history plays, sovereignty is something that is, indeed, much more like an endless process than something that is ever finite, or that could ever be finished: something that has more affinity with disarticulated body parts than with a stable and coherent 'body politic'. Christopher Pye's account of the political aesthetics of early modernity lead him in similar directions. 'As a political formation', he writes, 'early modern aesthetics retains the creationist emphasis of *poesis*, but a *poesis* become untethered from transcendent reference, or one that reflects back on and thus problematises the analogy with divine creation that governs it.'[12] This sense of 'untethering', a dislocation of political form from a supposed metaphysical origin, is both traced and enacted in Shakespeare's treatment of body parts in the history plays.

Another example from *Henry VI* part two might further illustrate the process.[13] This time we are in the scene in which Duke Humphrey's dead body is discovered, after he has been murdered in his bed. The body is brought on to the stage a couple of scenes after Margaret's accusations described above, and still in the section of the play most associated with Shakespeare. The account that Warwick gives of the corpse in the earlier play, *The First Part of the Contention*, is a straightforward, functional description of what has happened to the duke's body post-mortem:

> Oft have I seene a timely parted ghost,
> Of ashie semblance, pale and bloodlesse
> But loe the blood is settled in his face,
> More better coloured then when he liv'd,
> His well proportioned beard made rough and sterne,
> His fingers spred abroad as one that graspt for life,
> Yet was by strength surprisde, the least of these are probable,
> It cannot chuse but he was murthered.[14]

As with Queen Margaret's description of Humphrey's disobedience, the details are primarily in service of the narrative, and are evidentiary in status. That is, the description of what has happened to his body is offered as an explanation of events. The details of the body's post-mortem state are almost like a crime scene report, providing evidence for what must have happened from what can now be seen. And the speech has more perlocutionary than illocutionary force, designed as a specific cue for further action, rather than as an occasion for reflection on the present circumstance.

When, however, this speech is reshaped in the folio text, narrative efficiency gives way to a super-extended blazon, dramatic cues give way to lengthy monologue, and forensics give way to poetics:

> See how the blood is settled in his face.
> Oft have I seen a timely parted ghost
> Of ashy semblance, meager, pale, and bloodless,
> Being all descended to the labouring heart;
> Who, in the conflict that it holds with death,
> Attracts the same for aidance 'gainst the enemy;
> Which, with the heart, there cools, and ne'er returneth
> To blush and beautify the cheek again.
> But see, his face is black and full of blood;
> His eyeballs further out than when he lived,

Staring full ghastly like a strangled man;
His hair upreared, his nostrils stretched with struggling,
His hands abroad displayed, as one that grasped
And tugged for life and was by strength subdued.
Look on the sheets: his hair, you see, is sticking;
His well-proportioned beard made rough and rugged,
Like to the summer's corn by tempest lodged.
It cannot be but he was murdered here;
The least of all these signs were probable. (11.146–64)

The sense is the same, and the idea of a forensic discovery of the murder is also still there. But the description of the corpse is now extraordinarily rich, extravagant even. The folio text has taken one aspect of the earlier version – the way that the corpse's fingers are 'spred abroad' – and applied this outward motion to the whole body so that it all seems stretched to breaking point: the eyeballs 'further out than when he lived', 'His hair upreard', 'his nostrils stretched'. This is a much more impactful use of rhetorical *enargia*, and it ensures that whatever prop was being used for the corpse – whether a model or an effigy of some sort, or the body of the actor playing Humphrey – is more vividly real for the audience, and also for the readers of the folio text. Susan Zimmerman has named the stage corpse as something that tests the limits of representation – 'the indeterminate being that escapes signification' – and Shakespeare's language here skates along with this indeterminacy, refusing to pin the body down to any single, coherent meaning.[15] But, alongside this increased vibrancy, there is also a distancing effect that accompanies the overuse of extended and mixed metaphors. So, for example, the simile for Humphrey's ruffled beard – 'Like to the summer's corn by tempest lodged' ['*lodged*. beaten flat', OED v.5] – adds a discordant, potentially alienating note as we are taken away from the spectacle of a dead body to the idea of early summer crops beaten down in a storm. It is not clear how his beard being comparable, via simile, to a ruined summer crop can be used as evidence that he has been murdered. And the sheer weight of the multiple details of the body produce an effect that Simon Palfrey has identified as an 'instinct' in Shakespeare's writing, 'to split and double all phenomena, such that everything is shadowed by alternatives it cannot escape'.[16] His seemingly irrepressible urge to use *hendiadys* ('To blush and beautify the cheek'; 'black and full of blood'; 'rough and rugged') and other figures of amplification (the accumulative *synonimia* of 'meager, pale, and bloodless' for example) is in evidence not just here, but in all of these augmented speeches in the folio text. This book will argue that such splitting and doubling of the body, and of bodies in the history plays – both rhetorical and physical – is related to how sovereignty is conceived in the plays: alienable; not unitary; in pieces.

Lukas Erne reads processes of revision like this in other of Shakespeare's plays, including *Henry V*, as evidence that some of these texts are designed for different audiences, one to be performed and one to be read. The additional details in texts such as the folio text of *Henry VI* part two he reads as compensation for the lack of performing bodies.[17] The folio text of *Henry VI* part two is most like one of the 'readerly' texts that Erne characterises as an 'attempt to raise the literary respectability of playtexts'.[18] The persistent use of the common rhetorical practice of *copia* – the elaboration of an idea through numerous figurations – would support at least some sense of the folio text as written with a more self-consciously literary style. But given other imperatives for this kind of language, the way that metaphors of the body might work either to sustain or to unravel systems of political authority, and the complex imbrication of the prop of the dead body with the attenuated metaphors of the dialogue, then more than the text's literary status is at stake in the choices being made. As much as it might be a bid for more literary recognition, the obvious excessiveness of writing like that of the *Henry VI* part two folio text is perhaps better characterised in Palfrey's terms as testing the adequacy, and the limitations, of current thoughts, ideas and languages:

> It is an excess that speaks of the inadequacy of present symbolic orders and institutional definitions. It speaks for and to what may come – ideas, forms, and audiences – a promise that exceeds our possession, opening onto unfinished possibilities, whether culturally attested or frighteningly new.[19]

Erne's 'readerly' Shakespeare texts have more in common with a Derridean sense of *écriture* than Erne, or even Palfrey, would be likely to suggest. Over time, Shakespeare's use of this proliferating language to test the limits of prevalent understandings of sovereignty becomes more and more trenchant. Harry Berger Jr is closer than either Erne or Palfrey to describing the productive complicities of Shakespeare's complex literary language with the exigencies of performance, when he writes of the plays' dialogue that Shakespeare's '*écriture* is not merely metanarrative but antinarrative'.[20] What Berger sees as the 'dislocation of the speeches in textual space', their drift away from embodied performance, he explains as 'alternate ways to dismember the play'.[21] That is, the excesses of Shakespeare's language remain detached from the narrative imperatives of the action; they interrupt readers and audiences otherwise imagined to be seduced by the opaque, readerly effects of this dialogue. And, in the kinds of example in which I am interested, politicised metaphors of the body drift away from their original purpose; they disrupt the typically tidy, conservative analogies of the 'body politic' and, as an inevitable part of this drift, Shakespeare's language interrogates the multiple ways in which our bodies are captured by sovereign power.

## Beehives, the Body Politic and the Work of Analogy

The convoluted metaphors of the body that comprise Shakespeare's revisions to *Henry VI* part two are part of a more widespread resistance in the language of the history plays to what might be thought of as conservative 'body politic' metaphors. The image of the 'body politic', in which the whole of the human body is taken, in various ways, as an analogy for a working political system, tends to promote a conservative idea of stability, predicated on a form of sovereignty that is constant, permanent or at least self-enclosed and self-determining. Shakespearean poetics, however, resist such analogical ways of thinking, and this resistance gains critical traction in the area of political thought, given the preponderance of analogy as a mode of argumentation within that tradition. That is not to say that analogical thought is not occasionally given an airing in the history plays. It is, for example, present in Canterbury's famous speech to Henry in *Henry V*, where he develops the somewhat clichéd metaphor of the kingdom as a beehive, another discrete, self-enclosed and self-determining system. He describes bees as 'Creatures that by a rule in nature teach / The act of order to a peopled kingdom' (1.2.187–8). The point of Canterbury's metaphor is that the 'king' of the bees stays at home while the 'officers of sorts' travel abroad, occupied by their various duties, but always centrifugally linked to the authority of the king:

> Where some like magistrates correct at home
> Others like merchants venture trade abroad;
> Others like soldiers, armèd in their stings,
> Make boot upon the summer's velvet buds,
> Which pillage they with merry march bring home
> To the tent royal of their emperor,
> Who, busied in his majesty, surveys
> The singing masons building roofs of gold,
> The civil citizens kneading up the honey,
> The poor mechanic porters crowding in
> Their heavy burdens at his narrow gate,
> The sad-eyed justice with his surly hum
> Delivering o'er to executors pale
> The lazy yawning drone. (1.2.191–204)

Even as the sense of Canterbury's extended metaphor is all about the centralisation of power in the 'tent royal', the impression of the speech is of a world that is spinning out of Canterbury's (and the emperor's) control; he is not glorious or isolated but '*busied* in his majesty'. The length and variety of the speech compounds a sense of busyness spiralling out of control. The teeming proliferation of the various kinds of citizen bee detracts from the message of centred control. And, although we are reminded at the end of this list of the capital powers of a king who is able to condemn lazy bees to execution at the hands of 'executors pale', even this image tends to divert attention from, rather than confirm, the sovereign solitude of the king bee.

And then we remember from the previous scene of *Henry V* that Canterbury, giving this apparently conservative version of self-contained sovereignty, is really advancing his own interests and is hardly working for the king at all as he makes this speech, and so all of these overburdened metaphors crumble. It is no more than a mere convenience for Canterbury to insist on the absolute sovereignty of Henry as king, as he clearly acts in ways that contradict and undermine this professed belief. For Canterbury, the Church comes first. And so, the 'narrow gate' of the hive that barely admits the 'heavy burdens' of the workers is an apt image for Shakespeare's way with metaphor, both here and elsewhere. These bees, burdens and workers all double and proliferate, and this proliferation of things and images works against the putative unity of the 'emperor', self-absorbed and 'busy' rather than, say, splendid, 'in his majesty'.[22]

A probable source for Shakespeare's use of the common beehive metaphor is Thomas Elyot's *Book Named the Governor*. Elyot, like the Archbishop of Canterbury in *Henry V*, uses the beehive as an emblem of why, as he writes, 'That one sovereaigne governour ought to be in a publike weale.'[23] Elyot's beehive metaphor is, like Shakespeare's, extended. But it all works much more clearly within the centrifugal analogy of a centralising, inalienable sovereignty, and is much more plainly analogical in its conceptual pattern:

> the bee is lefte to man, as hit seemeth, a perpetuall figure of a juste governaunce or rule: who hath amonge them one principall bee for theyr governour, who excelleth all other in greatnes, yet hath he no prike or stinge, but in hym is more knowlege than in the residue. For if the day folowyng, shall be fayre and drye, and that the bees may issue out of theyr stalles without peryll of rayne, or vehement wynde, in the morning erely he calleth them, makyng a noyse as it were the sowne of a horne, or a trumpet, & with that, al the residue prepare them to labour, & fleeth abrode, gathering nothing, but that shall be swete and profitable, all though they sitte often tymes on herbes, & other thinges that be venomous & stynkinge. The capitayne laboureth nat

for his sustenance, but all the other for hym: he onely seeth, that if any drane or other unprofitable bee, entreth into the hyve, and consumethe the hony gathered by other, that he be immediately expelled from that company.[24]

Elyot ends on the same note of absolute sovereign decision making as Shakespeare in his version of the metaphor, albeit here it is exile rather than execution that acts as evidence of the monarch's absolutist decision-making capacities. What is lacking here, though, and what Shakespeare adds in his version of the metaphor, is the intense sense of teeming life that is achieved by piling metaphor on top of metaphor in a manner that thwarts the anchoring or 'keystone' tendencies of analogy or allegory.

If the baroque instantiates a movement away from analogical modes, then Canterbury's speech is, despite itself and the archbishop's best efforts, baroque. It might best be understood as a move away from the humanist scholar's use of careful analogy and towards the ruined forms of baroque allegory that Benjamin describes as '[piling] up fragments ceaselessly, without any strict idea of a goal'.[25] For Benjamin, the 'perfect vision' of a new baroque form of allegory that dispenses with specific metaphysical grounding is the ruin. Zimmerman explains the Benjaminian allegory as 'a mode of representation that disrupts the fantasy of coherence and continuity'.[26] Grady explains this as the birth of a particular form of fragmentary modern allegory: 'No longer organically unified, nature is open to allegoricisation in fragments. That is to say, the world loses any intrinsic meaning and becomes a set of hieroglyphs open to allegorical interpretation.'[27] If the figure of the ruin is the clearest example of this open-ended, fragmentary form of allegoricisation, particularly in the realm of history, then the fragmented body – the body in parts – is a corollary in the field of political thought. Shakespeare's baroque bodies move the political thought of the history plays towards what might be seen as baroque allegory, and away from the analogical ways of thinking that might typically be associated with the metaphor of the 'body politic'.

It was Michel Foucault who most influentially described the ways by which early modern thought could often work through analogy in *The Order of Things*, where he defines what he sees as the dominant sixteenth- and early seventeenth-century *episteme* (way of knowing about, and describing, the world) as constructed through forms of 'similitude'. For early moderns, he writes, 'The universe was folded in on itself.'[28] Analogy is one of Foucault's four types of similitude, the others being convenience (or adjacency), emulation and sympathy. All of these ways of seeing, and writing about, the world tend to be self-authorising, or self-authenticating. So, in the case of analogy – where the supposed truth of one system is explained by means of a description of another system

– explanations can always be reversed: 'An analogy may also be turned around upon itself without thereby rendering itself open to dispute.'[29]

Without any external guarantor of the truth of any description, analogies become self-enclosed. Foucault's early modern world of 'one vast single text' is, as he describes it, both 'plethoric' and 'poverty-stricken' at the same time.[30] The text of analogy can contain not just multitudes, but absolutely everything; at the same time, meaning is collapsed and erased into an impoverished world of endless self-replication. Analogy is the perfect vehicle for a form of sovereignty that is imagined as inalienable. The way that analogy works, as in Elyot's and Canterbury's beehive, through the relationships between micro- and macrocosm can seem as if they might be endlessly generative, but there are clear limitations to how this kind of thinking can treat complex political phenomena. 'Sixteenth-century knowledge', Foucault writes, 'condemned itself to never knowing anything but the same thing, and to knowing that thing only at the unattainable end of an endless journey.'[31] The way that Shakespeare's metaphors endlessly proliferate, with one thing always leading on to another – and another – might seem to work within Foucault's paradigm for early modern thought, in which 'the universe was folded in on itself'. But Foucault's 'folds' are not the baroque folds that Deleuze describes, and they are not the folds of language within which Shakespeare's multiplying body parts are articulated. The end of Foucault's 'endless' journey might be 'unattainable', but it exists in relation to an idea of the end, of a final position from which meaning is generated. Baroque forms have no such end, whether real, putative or constitutive. Canterbury's analogy *tries* to fold the world into the sovereign will of Henry, but the restlessness of Shakespeare's metaphorical way of writing tests the limits of 'similitude' as a way of understanding the world. Canterbury tries to be Foucauldian, but Shakespeare's poetics are too baroque. Most conceptions of sovereignty, in this period, are invested in ideas of centralised stability and tied to analogical modes of thought. But Shakespeare's writing consistently and agitatedly poses a challenge to this most fundamental use of analogy: the body politic.

To return briefly to his version of the beehive, Shakespeare's bees, as well as representing the workings of the court, are also 'merchants' who 'venture trade abroad', or soldiers making 'boot upon the summer's velvet buds'. The masons who build the golden palace are needlessly singing, and so on. All of these extraneous details – velvet buds and singing – are incidental to the allegorical, or analogical, intent of the speech. They also detract from it in a way that leaves behind the allegoricising capacities of centralising sovereignty. If unitary sovereignty depends on tributary relationships between parts and wholes and is often figured through homogenising metonymies in which multiple parts can be contained within singular wholes – what Foucault would call 'similitude' – then Shakespeare's metaphors, similes and metonymies run counter to these kinds of figuration. His 'similitudes' are not always so similar. They are, to put it mildly, always a little off kilter.

It is the work of this book to show how this tendency in Shakespeare's writing operates in the history plays' various treatments of human bodies, in part and in whole. The beehive is a popular analogy, in the early modern period, for the workings of the perfect monarchical state. However – from Jean Bodin's sovereign body through to Thomas Hobbes's artificial person of the 'Leviathan' – the body politic, the human body, offers much richer ground for political thought. Much less celebrated or important than Bodin or Hobbes, a typical example of the 'body politic' metaphor can be seen in a work of simple – simplistic even – political analogy, Edward Forsett's 1606 *A Comparative Discourse of the Bodies Natural and Politique*. The historian J. P. Somerville calls this short tract 'an idiosyncratic and rather foolish work', and not without some justification.[32] The book is, indeed, very basic in its uses of analogy. But it is hard to imagine anybody closer to the centre of Tudor and Stuart orthodoxy than Forsett who, upon graduating from Cambridge University in the early 1580s, went into royal service under the patronage of either William Cecil or Gilbert Gerard, Queen Elizabeth's Attorney General. By 1606, when he wrote his *Comparative Discourse*, he was working in the office of works at the Tower of London, shortly before being elected as Member of Parliament for Wells, Somerset. His was a career of consummate conservatism, never attracting controversy and ending up, in his old age, as a judge, no doubt 'full of wise saws and modern instances', dying at the age of 76.[33]

The conservatism of his career coincides with a stabilising tendency in his approach to language and metaphor. The opening passage of the dedication 'To the Reader' of the *Comparative Discourse* could stand as a model example of Foucault's analogical world, 'folded in on itself':

> The Commonweale with all her parts, orders, qualities, and requisites whatsoever, is (for better apprehension & illustration) set forth by sundry fit resemblances, as by the architecture of an house, by the swarming and cohabiting of Bees in an hive, by a ship floating on the sea, and such like; but by none more properly than eyther by the universall masse of the whole world, (consisting of all the severall subsistances in that great frame by the high wisdome and might of God compact and united) or else by the body of man, being the lesser world, even the diminitive and modell of that wide extending universall.[34]

Forsett operates within a world of knowledge that only knows itself, and with the micro- and macrocosmic relationship of the body of man to the 'universall masse of the whole world' as its organising principle. Beehives, ships and human bodies are all interchangeable in the analogically determined picture of sovereignty that he wants to paint; the paradoxical plenitude of a vision that is ultimately limited and impoverished is, in this paradigm of analogical thought, evident.

Forsett, at times, however, seems – notwithstanding his undoubted 'foolishness' – oddly conscious of the risks of misapprehension, or intellectual blindness, entailed in this type of analogical thought. A lot of his tract is spent overexplaining the implications of particular metaphors, in ways that suggest an attempt to guard against the possibility of divergent readings. One such elaborated metaphor understands sovereignty as the 'soul' or 'essence' of the state and the subject as the 'body' or the 'matter' upon which the soul works:

> Then as the soule is the forme which to the body giveth being, and essence; and the body is the matter which desiringly affecteth his forme: so both the ruler should wholy indevour the welfare of his people, and the subject ought (as in love to his owne soule) to conforme unto his soveraigne; that both of them mutually like twinnes of one wombe, may in the neere and deare nature of relatives, maintaine unviolate that compound of concordance, in which and for which they were first combined.[35]

This is not an unusual analogy to make, although the depiction of the soul and the body as 'mutually like two twines of one wombe' might be read as a simile that contradicts, rather than supports, the master and servant type relationship that Forsett elsewhere imagines for sovereign and subject. But, despite its being commonplace, Forsett seems aware of the problems of analogy, and attempts to head off any overly precious readings of his work. He cautions, in a pre-emptive way, against paranoid readings made by people who he calls 'makebates', who pick apart the details of his numerous metaphors of the body politic:

> It is easie for a curious objector, even in the fittest comparisons to make disseverance by inferring different respects and inequallitie. The dissimilitudes of things be infinite, and rometh with errour in the circumference, where the well apted likenesse setleth in the center of truth, and is compacted closely in one onely point of good congruitie, from the which it may neither be drawne awry without wrongfull wresting, nor enlarged too far without extreame torturing. It is the greatest miracle of Gods powerfull wisdome, in the innumerable formes of things, to make so infinite variation; Then it must needs be a great worke of the wit of man, in such multiplicitie of difference to find out the well agreeing semblances, To knit and match together sundry things by an aptnesse of application, is the proper effect of union; but to disjoyne the

well coupled from their lovely analogie of each to other, is a violent divorce and distraction: Therefore let such makebates (if any be) abate their humor of crossing with dissimilitudes, & content their conceits with that which they shall discerne to be matched with a right mirror, and representingly expressed by the shew of a good concordance.[36]

It is worth quoting in full Forsett's desperate plea for sympathetic readers who do not reveal themselves to be 'makebates' (fomenters of discord). First, this passage indicates some slight awareness on the part of one early modern writer of the limitations that Foucault identifies in their modes of thought: a coexistent plenitude ('multiplicitie of difference') and poverty ('well agreeing semblance') of ideas. Secondly, Forsett also reveals the particular difficulty attached to modes of analogy that centre on the human body, as the 'wit of man' is pitched against 'Gods powerfull wisdome' in an attempt to rein in the vast multiplicity of things with the human itself as measure. Lastly (and not least, for me), I find Forsett's anxiety helpful because I really want to be one of his awkward 'makebates', asking to 'make disseverance' in our understanding of, at least, Shakespeare's various uses of the human body in his depictions of the workings of sovereignty in the history plays. But even more importantly, Shakespeare's own metaphorical convolutions reveal him, also, as a potential 'makebate' whose writing works to dissever the metaphorical vehicle of the body from the tenor of sovereignty.

In early modern political theory, the metaphor of the body politic is often used to render the complex business of state politics more readily comprehensible. It is a metaphor 'we live by' in the sense meant by George Lakoff and Mark Johnson. 'Metaphors are conceptual in nature', they write, continuing that 'they play a central role in the construction of social and political reality'.[37] The use of the human body as an analogical measure, or metaphorical vehicle, can, however, be seen as something that disrupts the conceptual clarity of any description of the workings of sovereignty. And that is because the real, physical human body is precisely what is at stake within the machinery of sovereign power. It is like using the jaws of a mouse as a metaphorical image for the springing jaws of a mousetrap; the analogy is not separate from the thing itself. The 'body politic' (perpetual, immortal, ideational) could never be simple, or pure ideation; it is, rather, a metaphor that draws attention to itself by always collapsing the vehicle of the 'body' back into the tenor of real bodies. Again Forsett, for all his 'foolishness', seems almost aware of this as a problem, pre-empting complaints about his work with a claim that the 'politique Philosopher' is uniquely placed to make use of this 'compacted epitome' of man as measure of all things. If it is acceptable for mathematicians and natural philosophers to do this, he writes, then 'much more may the politique Philosopher, having for his proper subject the compound of men civilly assembled and associate, make man the object of his discourse and contemplation'.[38] Because humanity *is* the particular subject of political philosophy, then it makes sense to use the human body as a model, or a means of comparison.

This kind of tautology is, however, exactly what might become unravelled in the 'makebate' reading that dissevers the one from the other: the idea of the 'body politic' in theory from the multiple bodies of politics in action. Or, to put it another way, if the metaphor of the body politic is to be imagined as an equation, then there is never going to be any simple equivalency; there will always be a fleshy remainder. I am taking my cue from Eric Santner, who writes of the enduring power of these metaphors that they 'get a grip on the imagination of individuals and collectives because they are ultimately sustained by the "real stuff" of fantasy, by the dimension I have been calling the flesh'.[39] Santner argues that the metaphor of the 'body politic' is so enduringly compelling because it seems never quite to be sustainable *as* a metaphor without direct reference to flesh, bodies and to a human life that in some way exceeds the metaphor itself. The multiple body parts of Shakespeare's history plays participate in this economy of excessive figuration, operating both as a representation that constitutes a 'body politic' writ large on the stage, but also metonymically implicating the flesh that, as Santner writes, 'sustains' that representation.

### Flesh or Metaphor: the Humours and 'Bare Life'

The relationship between real, material bodies – Santner's 'fleshy' remainders – and the discourses through which they might be understood has been the focus of recent critical activity in early modern studies, particularly in two areas: first, the renewed attention paid to the material, often humoral, body inaugurated by Gail Kern Paster; and, secondly, in work derived from Giorgio Agamben's concept of 'bare life'. Emerging in apparently very different areas of early modern studies, both approaches nevertheless confront what might be thought of as bodies that are either in excess of, or unamenable to, figuration. As a result, this work is extremely useful for its reappraisal of what is at stake when early modern writers, including dramatists, write about human bodies, or use metaphors that are grounded in embodied experience. The approach that I am taking in this book is a particular and sustained focus on figuration, on metaphor and metonymy, and on Shakespeare's language, and might run counter to some of the dominant materialist tendencies in Shakespeare studies. Mine is a self-confessedly formalist approach. But an awareness of the lack of congruence between material bodies and the figures through which those bodies get co-opted by the workings of sovereign power remains at the heart of what I am doing; even as I turn my attention to form – to metaphor, metonymy and their uses alongside the performing bodies on Shakespeare's stage – the foundation of Shakespeare's metonymic body parts on real dissevered bodies remains a consideration.

Gail Kern Paster's influential re-evaluation of the passions and of humoral theory as being not, for the early moderns, merely a set of adaptable linguistic, conceptual or metaphorical structures but, rather, the basis upon which they actually experienced life is certainly a reminder of the limitations of analogical thought when it comes to the body. A foundational text, for Paster, is the mid-seventeenth-century tract, *Treatise of the Passions and Faculties of the Soule of Man*, by Edward Reynolds. Reynolds, Paster explains, understands the 'passions' as an integral part of the physical body, explicable by means of humoral theory. Moreover, the relationship between the passions and the physical humours is not, for Reynolds or for Paster, merely analogical:

> Reynolds . . . understands the nature of the passions as liquid – contained or uncontained, clear or muddy. The passions are like liquid states and forces of the natural world. But the passions – thanks to their close functional relation to the four bodily humors of blood, choler, black bile, and phlegm – had a more than analogical relation to liquid states and forces of nature. In an important sense, the passions actually *were* liquid forces of nature because, in this cosmology, the stuff of the outside world and the stuff of the body were composed of the same elemental materials.[40]

Paster emphasises the extent to which what might appear like a complex system of figurative and analogical thought, connecting colours with humours, passions and personalities, was taken literally by Shakespeare and his contemporaries. But Paster's importunate italics – 'the passions actually *were* liquid forces of nature' – reveal, despite themselves, the particular limitations of her argument and of this approach. These difficulties are further demonstrated as she immediately collapses supposedly physical phenomena – 'states and forces' – into a metaphorical and even a metaphysical schema: 'this cosmology'. That it is the verb, 'to be', that causes trouble for Paster ('passions . . . *were* . . . liquid forces') is a telling indication of the problems that might attend any claim that the humoral body could be fully anything other than a discursive construct, either for us or for early moderns. Paster wants the word to mean more than it usually does here, but there is no greater expression of identification than 'to be' in the English language and, as Paster seems to be aware, it always contains the shadows of a lack of equivalence as much as it forges correspondence. As Paster writes earlier in her paragraph, 'the passions are *like* liquid forces' (my emphasis). The passions are not actually liquid; they are 'like' liquid, a complex simile that precisely works within the structures of analogy that Paster then works hard to unravel. As James Knapp reminds us, contrary to the work of Paster, both Shakespeare and others were, in fact, profoundly interested in 'what lay beyond the senses and the material world'.[41] That is, Shakespeare is likely to be more interested in ideas to do with the body – what it can mean and how it is made to mean something within culture – than in its various fluids. He is always more interested in words than he is in anything else. How a body might seem like another thing is of more interest to him than what it *is*. Moreover, if we do not consider the ways that bodies become trammelled up in ideational systems – how bodies become metaphors and how those metaphors proliferate and break down – then we miss some of the ways in which a politics, founded in and impacting upon the human body, might work.

Recent work following the lead of the Italian political thinker, linguist and philosopher Giorgio Agamben might not seem connected to the quotidian materialism of Paster's humoral body. And, unlike much of the new materialism, it is work that very directly addresses the political implications of how bodies are represented. Unlikely partners though they might seem, both approaches share an interest in the near-inexpressible experience of embodiment as a ground zero around which analysis might circulate without ever managing to land. Daniel Juan Gil's work makes use of Agamben in interesting and productive ways as a means to uncover Shakespeare's concern with what he identifies as 'the phenomenological experience of utter subjection to sovereign power'.[42] Gil takes Agamben's reworking of Carl Schmitt's influential theories of sovereignty as his starting point. For Schmitt, sovereignty is generated from a singular presence that cannot be split up or divided. The necessary expression of Schmitt's version of indivisible sovereignty, ultimately derived from the early modern political theorist Bodin, is the 'state of emergency' in which any law that exists independent of the central sovereign power is suspended:

> The exception, which is not codified in the existing legal order, can at best be characterised as a case of extreme peril, a danger to the existence of the state, or the like. But it cannot be circumscribed factually and made to conform to a preformed law.[43]

Agamben takes up Schmitt's emphasis on the state of emergency, or on the exceptional decision, as the defining characteristic of sovereign power, and explores its implications. For Agamben, the 'state of exception' that collapses all law making into an extra-legal sovereign will cannot be contained within a particular historical moment but, rather, shadows all political life and action. 'The paradox of sovereignty', he writes, 'consists in the fact that the sovereign is, at the same time, outside and inside the juridical order.'[44] Similarly, the category of 'bare life' or '*homo sacer*', perhaps Agamben's best-known concept, is paradoxically both the product of specific legal circumstances and a form of life that lies outside the law's parameters. It is a form of life that is sometimes considered sacred but is denied protection or even categorisation under the law or within religious rituals. Through this delimitation, however, it is also the form of life whose existence confirms sovereignty's capacity to act, especially to exile or to execute. In the work of Agamben, decisionist sovereignty is intertwined with an understanding of human life as always vulnerable. 'The production of bare life is', he writes, 'the originary activity of sovereignty':

> We may even then advance a hypothesis: once brought back to his proper place beyond both penal law and sacrifice, *homo sacer* presents the originary figure of life taken into the sovereign ban and preserves the memory of the originary exclusion through which the political dimension was first constituted.[45]

For Gil, the figure (or lack of figure) of the *homo sacer* is anticipated in Shakespeare's work, particularly in the way that Shakespeare's bodies seem not to be easily contained within any particular form of social order. He argues that Shakespeare's version of sovereignty, like that theorised by Agamben, produces a residue of flesh that is in excess of any form of mediation:

> When it appears in Shakespeare's plays, sovereign power strips characters of their conventional social roles and identities and transforms them into a new and generative category of the flesh, capable of entering into new kinds of relationship with other flesh.[46]

Gil is writing about *Lear*, *Othello*, *Julius Caesar* and *Measure for Measure*. And that is, I think, significant. These plays present bodies in extreme, transformative circumstances. When, in the earlier history plays, Shakespeare turned his eye on the workings of the English crown, much less absolutist forms result. Gil's work, like that of Agamben, however much it resists the metaphysical, retains a sense of the ineffable. This reification of the body as a residual fleshiness that escapes inclusion within political forms and, for Gil, provides an escape from political life entirely is not sustainable in a reading of bodies in the history plays.

Here, the body is itself always in the process of becoming figured within sovereignty, flesh itself a metonymy for sovereign power. Bodies are always understood in relation to other bodies, or to objects, or to body parts: orb, crown, sceptre, neck, hand, knee and head.

## The Body Politic: Political Theory in the History Plays

What is at stake in these plays' uses of body parts is the extent to which sovereignty might be defined as something that is singular – a unified and unifying presence – and, contrarily, the extent to which it is, in fact, always liable to division. Shakespearean *poesis* leads us towards the latter – towards a form of sovereignty that is never complete, and never absolute. The otherwise powerful and ubiquitous metaphor, or analogy, of the 'body politic' is something that it is not possible to reconcile with the way that Shakespeare uses body parts in the dialogue and action of the English history plays. These plays are everywhere littered instead with parts of bodies, on the stage and in the dialogue, both literal and figurative. But they hardly ever imply anything like a unified body. Richard of Gloucester (the future Richard III) throws the severed head of Somerset on to the stage during the opening scene of *Henry VI* part three; 'hand' metaphors are repeated in a way that seems obsessive in *King John*; and the dialogue of *Henry V* contains multiple references to, and synonyms for, the 'neck' or the 'throat', necks that are cut, strangled or eroticised. As a corollary to these disparate body parts, the concept of sovereignty is neither imagined nor represented as staying still for very long. The idea of sovereignty is not given a fixed image through which it can come sharply into focus during any of the plays. Just as Queen Margaret, in common with many other characters, seems to struggle to contain her words, proliferating a seemingly endless supply of disjointed metaphors, the plays themselves never settle on a unifying image of sovereign power. Rather, sovereign power is something that is always itinerant, not resting easy in the hands of any one person or in any single object: neither in the solitary figures of particular kings nor in stage-props such as crowns, swords or letters. Shakespeare's history plays develop a distinctive understanding of sovereignty that sees it as something that is, rather, always mobile, as complicatedly produced and entangled in action and transaction: an order given or retracted; the picking up of a sword; a piece of paper read out or passed to somebody else.

The ten English history plays that Shakespeare either wrote in full or, as with the *Henry VI* plays and *Edward III*, had a share in writing were all written, and first performed, in the febrile political environment of the 1590s.[47] The political tensions of these last years of Elizabeth I's reign have been well documented and analysed. John Guy's description of this period as 'Elizabeth's second reign' marks it out as a time in which not just the individual circumstances of the English crown and its succession were the topic of intense debate, but the nature of sovereignty itself. The deteriorating political contexts within which the Elizabethan state was working (war with Spain; military intervention in the Netherlands; lack of clear succession to the throne; factional politics at court) resulted in widespread consideration being given to the mechanisms of political power and particularly to the status of sovereign power. In England, the more conciliar forms of rule that had characterised Elizabeth's earlier reign, referred to by Patrick Collinson as the Elizabethan 'monarchical republic', gave way to more authoritarian government.[48] In turn, as Guy argues, 'Writers became fascinated . . . by the themes of kingship, authority, and the acquisition and retention of power, particularly in relation to humanist-classical definitions of "virtue" in its civic and military aspects.'[49] He points towards the uptake of ideas derived from Tacitus in English political discourse, and a consequent focus on the potential for the corrupting influence of authoritarian rule. Alexandra Gajda demonstrates the ways in which such contexts cannot be contained within the period of 1585 to 1603 that Guy uses as his boundaries for the 'second reign', and shows how both authoritarian conceptions of monarchy, and resistance to them, were already available in the earlier periods of Elizabeth's reign. Gajda describes, instead, 'an increasingly diversified political culture' throughout the whole of Elizabeth's reign.[50] It is the case, however, that a politically charged interest in English history flourishes in the 1580s and 1590s. And, as Andrew Hadfield writes, given the political crises of these years, 'it is little wonder that plays dealing with English history should prove so popular with a theatre public'.[51] The problems with the Tudor succession could be seen to stretch back into the two centuries' worth of dynastic conflict depicted in Shakespeare's plays.

This unstable but highly energised time in English politics coincided with, and participated in, wider European conflicts over questions of sovereignty, conflicts that were played out in royal courts, on the battlefield and in print. The fight over the French crown that lasted the duration of the sixteenth century was particularly fertile for the dissemination of political argument and theory. On the one hand, the Huguenot experience led to the publication of the famous 1579 tract, the *Vindiciae Contra Tyrranos*, the most famous articulation of 'resistance theory', the right of subjects to reject tyrannical monarchy. On the other hand, the French wars of religion also provide the context within which the writings of Jean Bodin emerged, and his highly influential argument that locates an inalienable sovereign power within the singular figure of the monarch.[52] This bifurcated response to political turmoil – either a centrifugal movement towards more distributed agency or a centripetal movement towards the consolidation of power – is what drives early modern political theory as it attempts to make sense of both the religio-political conflicts of the period, and the rise of powerful courts centred on charismatic rulers. The twentieth-century political theorist Sheldon Wolin claims that periods of crisis are particularly conducive to the development of new political concepts. 'Most', he writes, 'of the great statements of political philosophy have been put forward in times of crisis.'[53] The idea is that the experience of chaos at times of political turmoil results in a search for solutions, for ways to restore order, to control uncertainty through theorisation. But that search itself, of course, only results in further contention as different writers arrive at quite different solutions.

The factionalism of early modern politics, and the consequent controversies of early modern political thought, could be characterised as an ongoing conflict between versions of the polity that sought unity, or that imagined either the state or the sovereign as self-defined, and other depictions of the state that leaned towards multiplicity. Bodin, in the *Six Livres*, theorises a form of sovereignty that can never be divided. As Julian Franklin writes, 'Bodin's principle of sovereignty ... is the assertion that there must exist, in every ordered commonwealth, a single centre of supreme authority and that this authority must necessarily be absolute.'[54] Bodin himself figures this as an inexhaustible sovereignty that can never be depleted, even as it might, at times, be forced to delegate: 'The person of the sovereign, according to the law, is always excepted no matter how much power and authority he grants to someone else; and he never gives so much that he does not hold back even more.'[55]

The phrase 'according to the law' is important here, indicating the way that Bodin derives his form of absolutism, not from a metaphysical grounding in an understanding of 'divine right' so much as it being a legal imperative. If there is going to be such a thing as sovereign power – and Bodin believes that there needs to be – then it is a legal (and logical) necessity that this power cannot be divided into parts but must be absolute; it must, in fact, be sovereign. It is interesting, however, that this most vehement theorist and defender of absolutism appears defensively to be responding to a wave of support on both sides of the French wars of religion for an understanding of sovereign power that was much more open to its division and dispersal. Quentin Skinner argues that Bodin anticipates Hobbes in his conclusion that it is both logically and legally essential for the legitimacy and perpetuation of any state for it to have, as its central motivating force, a singular, inalienable sovereignty:

> He [Bodin] is ... drawn by the logic of his own ideological commitment into arguing that in any political society there must be a sovereign who is absolute in the sense that he commands but is never commanded, and so can never be lawfully opposed by any of his subjects.[56]

J. H. M. Salmon and Ralph E. Giesey also argue that Bodin is responding to others, and particularly to Huguenot 'monarchomach' writers who were arguing that sovereignty should rest with the nation rather than the crown. They write that Bodin's 'doctrine of the indivisible legislative power of the French crown was defined in contradistinction to this implication in monarchomach thought'.[57] Bodin's reactionary absolutism exists in response to a wide variety of other possibilities. Not only were there the Huguenot writers who, in *Vindiciae Contra Tyrranos*, argued for the legitimacy of resisting tyrannical monarchs, there were other Protestant writers such as François Hotman who, in his *Francogallia*, argued determinedly for an elective monarchy. But ideas that rejected absolutist monarchy were not, in French political thought, restricted to the side of the Huguenots. Robert Persons, for example, an English-born Jesuit priest writing from exile in France, used resistance theory and arguments in favour of elective monarchy to promote the election of a Catholic successor to the English throne.[58]

Closer to home, critics have identified in the history plays an incipient republicanism that works against the apparent direction of the plays towards a vindication of the Tudor occupancy of the English throne. Like Gil, I am sceptical of any claims that Shakespeare's plays can be readily construed within the allegorical framework of a particular political programme. Gil argues that to see 'Shakespeare as a partisan of either absolutism or of civic republicanism misses the fundamentally anti-political drive in his literary-political imagination'.[59] But rather than see Shakespeare's resistance to allegoricisation or analogy as a form of 'nihilistic critique', I read his endlessly productive language as a form of political *poesis*.

The multiplicity of body parts in the history plays might prevent an absolutist version of sovereignty ever coming fully into view, but this need not be seen only as a form of negation. And while Shakespeare's highly figurative language might be too various to be reconciled with the formulae proposed for classical republicanism, that does not mean that the plays do not consider the possibilities of a variety of forms of political agency. Although this book takes a determinedly formalist approach, it is not an approach that is pursued in the absence of historical context. Nor are the two separate: the reification of social relationships into a political configuration is always, in part, a question of form.

And the forms assumed by prevailing political relationships in early modern England were not all necessarily centripetal, or oriented towards the centralised authority of the crown or the monarch. As explored by Henry Turner, the importance of the 'corporation' as a political form in early modern England suggests that the relationship between centralised unity and multiple pluralities was a dynamic one. Turner sees multiple corporate bodies (parliament, the judiciary, commercial enterprises, the crown and court) competing with each other within a burgeoning public arena where spheres of influence overlapped, rather than operating in a role subservient to a Bodin-like, authoritarian and centralising sovereign body. Early modern political forms fall away from Aristotelian norms within which 'the unity of the whole always precedes the part'.[60] Focusing on Sir Thomas Smith's important account of contemporary political systems, the *de Republica Anglorum*, written in 1565 but published in 1583, Turner sees a disjunction between the ideation of sovereign unity that occupied early modern political thought and the development of multiple sites of corporate capacity:

> Viewed philosophically, the English commonwealth resembles a species of corporate community in which one is composed out of many and many resolve into one; viewed historically or materially, this same commonwealth dissolves into the courts, officers, tables, documents, and grammatical formulas that bind the political community together by extending its way into everyday life.[61]

It seems clear to me that this question of the relationship of the one to the many, of the dissolution of sovereignty into plurality – what Turner refers to as 'the problems of unity and plurality, of person and group, of form and mimesis' – is in part a question both of form and of *poesis*, and of analogy giving way to an endless metaphorisation.

What I investigate in this book is the potential for the plays' poetics, their particular forms of *poesis* – uses of metaphor; the relationship between dialogue and staging – to make an intervention into political thought. If they do engage political theory, however, they do not do so in a way that advances a particular version of how the politics of sovereignty might, or could, work. Rather, the restless language of the plays continually imagines, or even brings into being, new political relationships, joining up and disarticulating bodies in a way that resists easy theorisation.

Victoria Kahn challenges us to understand Shakespearean politics through an appreciation of his investment in world creating, in *poesis*. She invites literary scholars to consider the work of twentieth-century political thinkers such as Carl Schmitt and Walter Benjamin precisely because they allow us to reconsider the role of literary criticism and its political purposes. 'This is', she writes, 'because they see *poesis* not simply as a literary question but also as an explicitly political question.'[62] Taking up Kahn's challenge with Shakespeare's history plays, I identify the plays' poetics, rather than their capacities to allegorise history, as a means through which a politics emerges that is not captured by the centrifugal forces of absolutism, or the teleological pull of political theology. This is not, then, political philosophy as understood by Wolin, in that it is absolutely not an attempt to recover order from chaos. However, the plays do still concern themselves with the legitimacy – and the limitations – of claims to sovereign power in ways that extend beyond the personal, or the immediately allegorical. They are not merely, or even, studies of the lives of individual monarchs so much as they are investigations into the implications of monarchical rule, investigations that are forged in dynamic acts of *poesis*. This process can be seen most clearly in the way that the plays deal with, represent, position and imagine the human body. Or, more particularly, how the defining metaphor of political thought – the body politic – gets radically rewritten over and over again ('fold after fold') in the language of these plays.

## Alienable Sovereignty and the Problem of Agency: 'Gimmers'

'Is the polis to be understood as a homogeneity', asks Turner,

> a 'one' made up of elements that are themselves undifferentiated as possible within themselves? Or does the unity of the polis contain a plurality of elements – each of which contains multitudes – even to the point where its unity is called into question?[63]

It is against the background of these questions that Shakespeare chooses, in his 1590s history plays, to represent sovereignty as characterised by a restless motility. This picture of restive and rootless power is particularly realised in the way that bodies – the sustained metaphor of the 'body politic' in particular – are reimagined in the history plays. Neither representations of the body nor ideas of sovereignty are ever unitary but are refracted and cut up. Richard II's broken mirror is only the most famous example of the way that the remediation of the king's body, in the history plays, is always one in which the 'brittle glory' of sovereignty is 'cracked in an hundred shivers' (4.1.A134–5). To the extent that there is a prevailing understanding of sovereignty that it should form some kind of unitary authority – an authority that inheres in a body politic that is indivisible – then Shakespeare's English history plays stage an incessant and seemingly inevitable unravelling of that idea or ideal.

Jacques Derrida writes that 'A pure sovereignty is indivisible or it is not at all, as all the theoreticians of sovereignty have rightly recognised', but goes on to explain that to think, write and theorise sovereignty, to represent it in some way, is always 'to compromise its deciding exceptionality':

> It is thus to divide it, to subject it to partitioning, to participation, to being shared. It is to take into account the part played by sovereignty. And to take that part or share into account is to turn sovereignty against itself, to compromise its immunity. This happens as soon as one speaks of it in order to give it or find in it some sense or meaning. But since this happens all the time, pure sovereignty does not exist ...[64]

Derrida, with customary precision, confutes a long tradition of thinking about sovereignty, the beginnings of which are frequently traced to the sixteenth century, or to early modernity more generally. From the sixteenth-century French jurist Bodin, through to the twentieth-century Nazi apologist Schmitt, to the contemporary Italian philosopher Agamben, there is a strong tradition in Western political thought that identifies sovereignty with the idea of the 'exception', and with forms of decisionism. Sovereignty, in this tradition, is located in the body (real or metaphorical) that has the unique and, importantly, inalienable capacity to decide without reference to others. Derrida's axiomatic pronouncement, 'A pure sovereignty is indivisible or it is not at all', affects, through its indeterminate grammar and logic, a form of deconstruction of the idea of '*pure* sovereignty'. Jacques Lezra lists some possible ways to parse Derrida's sentence:

> 'Pure sovereignty,' the little logical table undergirding Derrida's argument might run, 'is invisible or it is not (sovereignty),' an ontological claim; 'pure sovereignty is indivisible or it is not (pure),' a Platonic claim; 'pure sovereignty is indivisible or it is not (indivisible),' a claim having the form of the basic logical necessity $P$ is $S$ or it is not $S$; in no case can $P$ be both $S$ and not-$S$.[65]

Lezra's careful reading of this passage from *Rogues* is part of his account of the politics of terrorism and/or of terror wherein he investigates claims made by theorists of sovereignty that, for power to remain 'sovereign', it cannot be divided. The implication is that sovereignty never has been – never could be – 'pure' or indivisible. The exceptional autonomy of the sovereign body is not something that could ever be realised.

In the abdication scene of *Richard II*, before Richard gets hold of the mirror, and just as he hands over the crown, he has some remarkable lines:

> I give this heavy weight from off my head,
> And this unwieldy sceptre from my hand,
> The pride of kingly sway from out my heart.
> With mine own tears I wash away my balm,
> With mine own hands I give away my crown,
> With mine own tongue deny my sacred state,
> With mine own breath release all duteous oaths. (4.1.145A50–6)

Richard takes verbal possession of his own body parts ('mine own … mine own') at the very moment when it is revealed that his possession of the crown has not afforded him any such autonomy. The emphatic anaphora of 'With mine own' is belied by the sense that he is not able to claim any real control over his own body. It has been, as it is now, always in the hands of others. Throughout his abdication speech Richard is, to use Derrida's words, 'taking account of the part played by sovereignty'. But in doing so – in wrestling his words into an apparent insistence on a renewed sovereignty of will, and into imagining an exceptional autonomy – that process of taking account also pulls the king's brittle body apart, refracting it through 'an hundred shivers' even before the mirror lies shattered on the ground.

Even as early modern political theorists begin to locate sovereignty, understood as the capacity to make sovereign decisions, in the variously imagined person of the monarch, the nation-states that were developing in the early modern period nevertheless depended upon multiple different, often competing, sets of obligations and agencies. Shakespeare's oblique response to the urgency of this debate is to present a sequence of histories in which, while they focus relentlessly on the person of the king, sovereignty is, itself, never localised. On fleeting occasions the figure of an individual, isolated king seems momentarily invested with the kind of exemplary pathos that might attach itself to the unique solitude of an absolute sovereignty: Richard II talking to himself on a Welsh beach after he returns from Ireland, or Henry V all alone on the night before Agincourt. But these moments do not last and are always surrounded and constrained by actions that unravel the briefly gathered-together autonomy of the individual kings.

Laurie Shannon has demonstrated that early modern conceptions of sovereignty are often characterised by a solitude that seems inescapable, an inevitable eschewal of the political sociabilities of friendship and companionability:

> Friendship theory and its faith in decorous parity, along with monarchy theory's interpolating exaltation of the sovereign and demand for the subordination of his private self, converged precisely to one effect: affectively speaking, they rendered the proper sovereign solitary.[66]

This sovereign solitude is one consequence of dominant early modern political theories that imagine sovereignty as locatable in an indivisible body. For early modern political thought, the leading expression of this idea comes in the work of Bodin. Quentin Skinner claims Bodin as the most significant political thinker of the period, writing that Bodin's *Six Books of the Commonweal* 'was arguably the most original and influential work of political philosophy to be written in the sixteenth century'.[67] The restless political atmosphere of the French wars of religion produced multiple investigations into the configurations of the state, of the monarchy, and of the concept of sovereignty, and Bodin's ideas were also avidly consumed in England. There, disputes over the nature of monarchy or sovereignty might have been a little more buried beneath the surface, given the relative stability of the Tudor state in comparison to the situation in Bodin's native France, but the politics of inheritance and of the legal status of the crown were just as critical as they were across the channel. Skinner cites Gabriel Harvey's observation that it was barely possible to 'step into a scholar's study' in the later years of Elizabeth I's reign without finding that scholar buried in their copy of Bodin.[68] What they would have been finding out about Bodin's view of sovereignty was his firm conviction that it needed to be both unified and absolute: indivisible.

Shakespeare's pursuit of a sovereignty that is, as it turns out, endlessly alienable results in some problems with sovereign agency in his plays. This is true even of those parts of *Henry VI* part one that seem to feature an English heroism that is most in the service of the sovereign authority of the king: the events surrounding the mighty Talbot. In the second scene of the play, the French are initially sceptical about the chances of the English army being able to maintain their siege of Orleans. Talbot, the talismanic English hero, has been captured and, after months without the sustenance of 'porridge' and 'fat bull-beeves', the French claim that the English must be starving (1.2.9). But their scepticism is unwarranted and, when they try to break up the English, the French are driven back. Initially characterising the English soldiers as 'desperate' and 'hare-brained', the most striking description is given by Reignier, Duke of Anjou, as he tries to account for their seemingly impossible persistence:

> I think by some odd gimmers or device
> Their arms are set, like clocks, still to strike on;
> Else ne'er could they hold out so as they do. (1.2.41–3)

'Gimmers' is an odd word, unavailable elsewhere in the work of Shakespeare or of Nashe, Shakespeare's co-writer on this play. It is a word for a hinge or bracket in a piece of machinery, a mechanism for transferring energy into motion. Reignier is claiming that the English must be mechanical, that they are a kind of automata. Unstoppable and without the fuel of Talbot and beef, they must surely be machines.

Brooke Conti writes that 'Animated objects, by their very nature, raise questions about agency and motivation.'[69] She is writing about a particularly famous late medieval/early modern automaton known as the Rood of Boxley, a crucifix that housed a Christ figure whose head and eyes could move. Protestant writers would attack such objects as examples of what they saw as the empty, purely mechanical nature of Catholic beliefs and practices. Joseph Hall wrote to James VI and I's son, Prince Henry, about the Rood of Boxley, calling it the 'Kentish Idol' that 'mooved his eies, and hands, by those secret gimmers, which now every Puppet-play can imitate'.[70] The word 'gimmers', as in *Henry VI* part one, indicates seemingly motiveless action, motion without agency.

This idea of action that is the result of an indiscernible, or even totally absent, agency is also represented in *Henry VI* part one in the rescue of Talbot from the house of the Countess of Auvergne. This whole scene is rather an odd inclusion in the play in that it is seemingly unnecessary for the plot. However, what it does provide is further meditation on the disconnection of action from the actor. The countess begins work on this disconnection when she first sees Talbot, finding him to be an enormous disappointment in comparison to the legend that had attracted her to him:

> I thought I should have seen some Hercules,
> A second Hector, for his grim aspect
> And large proportion of his strong-knit limbs.
> Alas, this is a child, a silly dwarf.
> It cannot be this weak and writhled shrimp
> Should strike such terror into his enemies. (2.3.18–23)

Regardless of the extent to which the body of the actor playing Talbot does or does not match either the countess's description or his image as a 'second Hector', these lines comically draw attention to a dislocation of the body from its description. When the countess lets Talbot know that her purpose in luring him to her house is to hold him prisoner, the scene continues to ask probing questions about the relationship between the body of Talbot and its representation. The countess has, until now, only had a portrait of Talbot to entertain her:

> Long time thy shadow hath been thrall to me,
> For in my gallery thy picture hangs;
> But now thy substance shall endure the like,
> And I will chain these legs and arms of thine
> That hast by tyranny these many years
> Wasted our country ... (2.3.35–41)

Talbot picks up on the way that the countess plays with ideas of representations and shadows, laughing that she still only has the 'shadow of myself':

> You are deceived: my substance is not here.
> For what you see is by the smallest part
> And least proportion of humanity.
> I tell you, madam, were the whole frame here,
> It is of such a spacious lofty pitch
> Your roof were not sufficient to contain't (2.3.51–6)

The answer to this riddle – the riddle of a Talbot who both is and is not fully contained by his own body – comes when he blows his horn and, seemingly from nowhere, a group of English soldiers enter the stage, coming to his rescue. These, Talbot says (talking about himself in the third person), 'are his substance, arms, and strength, / With which he yoketh your rebellious necks' (2.3.63–4). The countess is forced to admit that 'thou art no less than fame hath bruited, / And more than may be gathered by thy shape' (2.3.68–9).

This short, mostly comic interlude is primarily designed further to impress upon the audience Talbot's capacities as an English hero, here effecting a narrow escape from a dreadful fate with the help of his loyal men. However, the dialogue throughout the scene continually draws attention to a mismatch between the body of the hero and the means – the shadows – by which he might be represented: the portrait, the body of the actor and, most notably, his extended body which now incorporates his soldiers. This play has a tendency to deal with sovereign agency by means of blazon, beginning with a description of the dead Henry V in the opening scene, through to the seemingly separable sinews and arms of Talbot in this scene. The effect of this is to dislocate agency from individual, unified bodies. In as much as the metaphor of the 'body politic' is in operation in *Henry VI* part one, it is a body that is open to dismemberment.

This is something that recurs throughout Shakespeare's English histories. Even as they tell the story of the transfer of power from one king to another, the body parts that litter their stages provide an image of resistance to the idea of a unitary sovereignty. The mechanistic and attenuated way in which bodies are imagined as being held together, or articulated, by 'gimmers' predates, but also predicts, the Hobbesian model of artificial sovereignty. In the *Henry VI* plays, these ideas circulate around the vacuum of a king who is largely absent from any of the action. In the other history plays – the two other Henrys, the two Richards and *King John* – Shakespeare turns his audiences' and readers' attention to the figures of individual kings.

## Notes

1. The full title is *The First part of the Contention betwixt the two famous Houses of Yorke and Lancaster, with the death of the good Duke Humphrey: And the banishment and death of the Duke of Suffolke, and the Tragicall end of the proud Cardinall of Winchester, with the notable Rebellion of Jacke Cade: And the Duke of Yorkes first claime unto the Crowne*. Hereafter referred to as *The First Part of the Contention*.
2. Gary Taylor and Rory Loughnane's conspectus of the textual evidence in the 'Authorship Companion' volume of the *New Oxford Shakespeare* offers a useful breakdown of how the complex layers of authorship and revision might be understood in this play; Gary Taylor and Rory Loughnane, 'The Canon and Chronology', in William Shakespeare, *The New Oxford Shakespeare* (Authorship Companion), ed. Gabriel Egan and Gary Taylor (Oxford: Oxford University Press, 2017), pp. 496–9. See also Hugh Craig, 'The Three Parts of *Henry VI*', in Hugh Craig and Arthur Kinney (eds), *Shakespeare, Computers, and the Mystery of Authorship* (Cambridge: Cambridge University Press, 2012), pp. 40–77.
3. Roland Greene, *Five Words: Critical Semantics in the Age of Shakespeare and Cervantes* (Chicago: University of Chicago Press, 2013), p. 161.
4. Anonymous, *The First Part of the Contention Betwixt the Two Famous Houses of Yorke and Lancaster, with the Death of the Good Duke Humphrey, and the Banishment and Death of the Duke of Suffolke, and the Tragicall End of the Proud Cardiall of Winchester, with the Notable Rebellion of Jacke Cade* (London, 1594), sig. D3v.
5. All references to, and quotations from, the texts of plays by Shakespeare, unless stated otherwise, are taken from William Shakespeare, *The New Oxford Shakespeare* (Modern Critical Edition), ed. Gabriel Egan and Gary Taylor (Oxford: Oxford University Press, 2016).
6. Walter Benjamin, *The Origin of German Tragic Drama*, trans. John Osborne (London: Verso, 1998), pp. 78–9.
7. Benjamin, *The Origin of German Tragic Drama*, p. 66.
8. See Hugh Grady's book on Donne and the baroque for an account of the productive work of periodisation that is implied by the labile term the 'baroque'; Hugh Grady, *John Donne and Baroque Allegory* (Cambridge: Cambridge University Press, 2017).

9. Gilles Deleuze, *The Fold: Leibniz and the Baroque*, trans. Tom Conley (Minneapolis: University of Minnesota Press, 1993), p. 33.
10. Philip Lorenz, *The Tears of Sovereignty: Perspectives of Power in Renaissance Drama* (New York: Fordham University Press, 2013), p. 16.
11. Deleuze, *The Fold*, p. 34.
12. Christopher Pye, *The Storm at Sea: Political Aesthetics in the Time of Shakespeare* (New York: Fordham University Press, 2015), p. 30.
13. It would be an extremely lengthy process to detail all of the examples from *Henry VI* part two in which Shakespeare reimagines sovereign relations through images of dispersed body parts; there are just so many of them, particularly in the expansions that characterise the folio. They include, for example, what is originally a simple soliloquy from York, outlining the plot point that he has 'seduste a headstrong Kentishman, / John [Jack] Cade of Ashford' (sig. E1v) to instigate a rebellion on his behalf. In the folio text, this becomes a much lengthier outline of his position as rebel, where he talks about his 'royal heart' in almost the same breath as he describes his 'brain, more busy than the laboring spider' and compares his subterfuge to 'the starvèd snake, / Who, cherished in your breasts, will sting your hearts' (9.336–46). None of these body parts or animals feature in the dialogue of the *The First Part of the Contention* but all are added as Shakespeare elaborates the text.
14. *The First Part of the Contention*, sig. E3r.
15. Susan Zimmerman, *The Early Modern Corpse and Shakespeare's Theatre* (Edinburgh: Edinburgh University Press, 2005), p. 18.
16. Simon Palfrey, *Shakespeare's Possible Worlds* (Cambridge: Cambridge University Press, 2014), p. 33.
17. Lukas Erne, *Shakespeare as Literary Dramatist* (Cambridge: Cambridge University Press, 2003).
18. Erne, *Shakespeare as Literary Dramatist*, p. 220.
19. Palfrey, *Shakespeare's Possible Worlds*, p. 40.
20. Harry Berger Jr, *Making Trifles of Terrors: Redistributing Complicities in Shakespeare* (Stanford: Stanford University Press, 1997), p. 129.
21. Berger, *Making Trifles of Terrors*, p. 102. Berger continues that 'it isn't clear to me that the former [speeches as distributed between performers in a performance] should have absolute priority over the latter [speeches as available, "dismembered", in a text-to-be-read]'.
22. 'Majesty' is a particularly telling word here. It is the word that Jean Bodin uses ('majesté') to define the self-determining and inalienable nature of sovereignty in the *Six Livres de la République*. While I go on to discuss Bodin in broad terms in this Introduction, I discuss Shakespeare's use of the word 'majesty' in relation to Bodin in the chapter on *King John*.
23. Thomas Elyot, *The Book Named the Governour* (London, 1531), sig. A6r.
24. Elyot, *The Book Named the Governour*, sig. A8r.
25. Benjamin, *The Origin of German Tragic Drama*, p. 178.
26. Zimmerman, *The Early Modern Corpse*, p. 14.
27. Grady, *John Donne and Baroque Allegory*, p. 49.
28. Michel Foucault, *The Order of Things: An Archaeology of the Human Sciences* (London: Routledge, 1970), p. 19.
29. Foucault, *The Order of Things*, p. 24.

30. Foucault, *The Order of Things*, pp. 38, 33–4.
31. Foucault, *The Order of Things*, p. 34.
32. J. P. Somerville, *Royalists and Patriots: Politics and Ideology in England 1603–1640* (London: Longman, 1999), p. 53.
33. 'Sir Edward Forsett', *Oxford Dictionary of National Biography*.
34. Edward Forsett, *A Comparative Discourse of the Bodies Natural and Politique wherein out of the Principles of Nature, is set forth the True Forme of a Commonweale, with the Dutie of Subiects, and Right of Soveraigne: together with many Good Points of Politicall Learning, mentioned in a Briefe after the Preface* (London, 1606), sig. ¶3r.
35. Forsett, *A Comparative Discourse*, sig. B2r–v.
36. Forsett, *A Comparative Discourse*, sig. ¶4v–A1r.
37. George Lakoff and Mark Johnson, *Metaphors We Live By* (Chicago: University of Chicago Press, 1980), p. 159.
38. Forsett, *A Comparative Discourse*, sig. B1v.
39. Eric Santner, *The Royal Remains: The People's Two Bodies and the Endgames of Sovereignty* (Chicago: University of Chicago Press, 2011), p. 43.
40. Gail Kern Paster, *Humoring the Body: Emotions and the Shakespearean Stage* (Chicago: University of Chicago Press, 2004), p. 4.
41. James A. Knapp, 'Beyond Materiality in Shakespeare Studies', *Literature Compass* 11.10 (2014), p. 684.
42. Daniel Juan Gil, *Shakespeare's Anti-Politics: Sovereign Power and the Life of the Flesh* (New York: Palgrave Macmillan, 2013), p. 1.
43. Carl Schmitt, *Political Theology: Four Chapters on the Concept of Sovereignty*, trans. George Schwah (Chicago: University of Chicago Press, 2005), p. 6. Schmitt's text was originally published in 1922.
44. Giorgio Agamben, *Homo Sacer: Sovereign Power and Bare Life*, trans. Daniel Heller-Roazen (Stanford: Stanford University Press, 1998), p. 15.
45. Agamben, *Homo Sacer*, p. 83.
46. Gil, *Shakespeare's Anti-Politics*, p. 6.
47. I am including *Edward III* here, but not *Henry VIII*, which strikes me as a very different kind of play.
48. Patrick Collinson, 'The Monarchical Republic of Elizabeth I', *Bulletin of the John Rylands University Library of Manchester* 69.2 (1987), pp. 394–424.
49. John Guy, 'Introduction: the 1590s: The Second Reign of Elizabeth I?', in John Guy (ed.), *The Reign of Elizabeth I: Court and Culture in the Last Decade* (Cambridge: Cambridge University Press, 1995), p. 15.
50. Alexandra Gajda, 'Political Culture in the 1590s: The "Second Reign" of Elizabeth', *History Compass* 8.1 (2010), p. 95.
51. Andrew Hadfield, *Shakespeare and Renaissance Politics* (London: Bloomsbury Arden Shakespeare, 2004), p. 41.
52. Quentin Skinner writes that Bodin's *Six Livres*, in which he articulated his theory of indivisible sovereignty, 'was, arguably, the most original and influential work of political philosophy to be written in the sixteenth century'; Quentin Skinner, *The Foundations of Modern Political Thought, Volume 1: The Renaissance* (Cambridge: Cambridge University Press, 1978), p. 208.
53. Sheldon S. Wolin, *Politics and Vision: Continuity and Innovation in Western Political Thought* (Princeton: Princeton University Press, 2016), p. 9. This

2016 'Princeton Classics' edition is based on the 2004 expanded version of his classic 1960 account of the history and development of political thought.
54. Julian Franklin, *Jean Bodin and the Rise of Absolutism* (Cambridge: Cambridge University Press, 1973), p. 23.
55. Jean Bodin, *On Sovereignty: Four Chapters from The Six Books of the Commonwealth*, ed. and trans. Julian H. Franklin (Cambridge: Cambridge University Press, 1992), p. 2.
56. Quentin Skinner, *The Foundations of Modern Political Thought, Volume 2: The Age of Reformation* (Cambridge: Cambridge University Press, 1978), p. 287.
57. J. H. M. Salmon and Ralph E. Giesey, 'Introduction', in François Hotman, *Francogalia*, ed. Ralph E. Giesey, trans. J. H. M. Salmon (Cambridge: Cambridge University Press, 1972), p. 93.
58. Robert Persons, *A Conference About the Next Succession to the Crown of England* (St Omer, 1594). A Jesuit priest, Persons published this anonymously. It was banned in England, although copies were imported. I discuss some aspects of this in the chapter on the *Henry IV* plays.
59. Gil, *Shakespeare's Anti-Politics*, p. 1.
60. Henry S. Turner, *The Corporate Commonwealth: Pluralism and Political Factions in England 1516–1651* (Chicago: University of Chicago Press, 2016), p. 9.
61. Turner, *The Corporate Commonwealth*, p. 57.
62. Victoria Kahn, *The Future of Illusion: Political Theology and Early Modern Texts* (Chicago: University of Chicago Press, 2014), p. 8.
63. Turner, *The Corporate Commonwealth*, p. 9.
64. Jacques Derrida, *Rogues: Two Essays on Reason*, trans. Pascale-Anne Brault and Michael Naas (Stanford: Stanford University Press, 2005), p. 101.
65. Jacques Lezra, *Wild Materialism: The Ethic of Terror and the Modern Republic* (New York: Fordham University Press, 2010), p. 70.
66. Laurie Shannon, *Sovereign Amity: Figures of Friendship in Shakespearean Contexts* (Chicago: University of Chicago Press, 2002), p. 155.
67. Skinner, *Foundations of Modern Political Thought*, vol. 1, p. 208.
68. Skinner, *Foundations of Modern Political Thought*, vol. 2, p. 300.
69. Brooke Conti, 'The Mechanical Saint: Early Modern Devotion and the Language of Automation', in Wendy Beth Hyman (ed.), *The Automaton in English Renaissance Literature* (Farnham: Ashgate, 2011), p. 98.
70. Joseph Hall, *Epistles* (London, 1608), p. 57.

Chapter 1

# Richard II as Robinson Crusoe: Sovereignty and the Impossibility of Solitude

> Sometimes our theorists confuse all the parts and sometimes they separate them. They make the sovereign a creature of fantasy, a patchwork of separate pieces, rather as if they were to construct a man of several bodies – one with eyes, one with legs, the other with feet and nothing else.[1]

Shakespeare's English history plays stage the incessant unravelling of an ideal version of sovereignty that would see it as inalienable. King, crowns, kingdoms: none of these are inviolable in the dialogue and action of these plays. However, for short-lived moments, the plays do sometimes isolate a king, placing him alone on stage. And this figure of an individual, isolated king becomes invested with a kind of exemplary pathos that could attach itself to the unique solitude of an absolute sovereignty: Henry V all alone on the night before Agincourt, or Richard II talking to himself on a Welsh beach after he returns from Ireland. And, as Laurie Shannon has demonstrated, early modern conceptions of sovereignty are often characterised by an inescapable and solipsistic solitude, the result of being forced to eschew the important political sociabilities of friendship and companionability:

> Friendship theory and its faith in decorous parity, along with monarchy theory's interpolating exaltation of the sovereign and demand for the subordination of his private self, converged precisely to one effect: affectively speaking, they rendered the proper sovereign solitary.[2]

Shakespeare's fleeting images of kings who appear immured in melancholic solitude are, however, always revealed to be fragile and inadequate metaphorical vehicles for the tenor of sovereignty. As Michael Harrawood argues about the particularly solitary Henry VI in *Henry VI* part three, it is partly Henry's incapacity to engage the world that leads to a failure in his authority. His language increasingly locates the source of his power within his own body, rather than in external things: 'My crown is in my heart, not on my head [. . .] / Not to be seen. My crown is called content' (3.1.60–2). Harrawood points out that this retreat, which is both real and symbolic, into the supposedly inviolable body of the self-sustaining monarch results not in a secure location for sovereignty but in its eventual dissipation:

> And having semiotically cut himself off from the political implications of his crown, he is now 'content,' that is—to take his word literally—contained within the private space of his own body. But the king's self-containment marks also his failure to sway.[3]

Also revealed in Henry VI's speech is that sovereign will, rather than being dependent on the splendid isolation of the king or prince, always requires the use of objects, especially weapons and pieces of writing, as well as sceptres, orbs and, here, crowns. Even as he attempts to negate the world of politics, Henry can't manage without the metaphor, or metonymy, of the 'crown'.

Even more necessary than these objects is the inescapable presence of other people. John Michael Archer shows how the imagined and idealised solitude of the early modern monarch seems to provide a model for agency in early modern essayists such as Montaigne, whose work has been seen as a forcing house for modern concepts of a self-possessed subjectivity. He writes that 'The friendless monarch's solitude serves as the pattern for developing individuality, a pattern that Montaigne tentatively usurps.'[4] However, as Archer also points out, this image of selfhood is far from stable, either for the imagined sovereign or for the essayist:

> Sovereignty, however, was not really the locus of a unitary and thoroughly autonomous power. Perhaps it became one of the prime models for individuality in the sixteenth century because it exemplified an instability and inscrutability similar to that ascribed to the developing self by a developing self-examination such as we find in the *Essais*.[5]

The solipsism both of the self-scrutinising essayist and of the solitary sovereign produces a fractured and unstable agent. Drama, however, affords further possibilities for exploring the sovereign solitude of the monarch. Solitude, on stage or in a theatre, is simply impossible. If Henry VI, or Richard II, or Henry V, is occasionally depicted as attempting to locate sovereignty within an increasing interiority, others constantly overrun the attempt. By presenting not just one 'body politic' but multiple interrelated bodies, the stage confutes an image of sovereignty as unitary. And so, if the abstract concept of sovereignty is embodied on Shakespeare's stage, it is located in movements and in exchanges between *parts* of bodies: hands grabbing swords; knees bending in supplication; tongues speaking words that have been borrowed from elsewhere; throats laid bare to violent attack. And the metaphors and metonymies that, in the dialogue of the history plays, both describe and contend sovereignty are equally fragmentary. From the blazon of the dead Henry V spoken over his coffin at the start of *Henry VI* part one, through to the constant harping on 'hands' and 'knees' that becomes a regular refrain of *Richard II*'s dialogue, and to the animal-suffused imagery of *Richard III*, Shakespeare's histories stage the pulling apart of any singular bodily container for sovereign power. In these plays, sovereignty is always in the process of being disarticulated from the persons of king and subject, which are only apparently discrete entities. 'Ultimately', Harrawood argues, 'the similes that express the body, the body politic, and the leadership models that serve it, all fail or refuse to create the unities implied by the likenesses they represent.'[6] The entanglement of persons and actions in the performances of the history plays has, then, a counterpart in the dialogue, and in metaphor and synecdoche. Shakespeare's uses of figurative language and a particular partiality that he has for bodily metamorphosis as a key troping mechanism result in his plays discovering a version of sovereign power that has it always on the move, only ever available in different kinds of shifting transaction.

Philip Lorenz writes that 'We think sovereignty . . . with and through its tropes' and that 'the most recurring of these tropes is the figure of the "body"'.[7] The Shakespearean body throughout the canon (from Bottom's transformation into a half-man/half-donkey in *A Midsummer Night's Dream* through to Hermione turning into a statue and back again in *The Winter's Tale*) is characteristically one that is in some kind of transit or metamorphosis. The text that most fascinated Shakespeare was Ovid's *Metamorphoses*. The *Metamorphoses* informs the way that much Renaissance literature thinks about how bodies might relate to each other and, in the process, renders bodily relations utterly strange. As Lynn Enterline writes, 'Fractured and fragmented bodies from Ovid's poem cast long, broken shadows over European literary history.'[8] Shakespeare's 1590s history plays might not be the texts that immediately spring to mind when thinking about those long Ovidian shadows; they tend to sideline erotic attachment as a primary concern, and an investigation of erotic desire is clearly the main motivation behind Shakespeare's and others' fascination with Ovid. But the history plays dominate Shakespeare's theatrical output in the 1590s and, at the same time, this is the decade that witnesses a high point in Ovidian literature in English, not least with Shakespeare's own two narrative poems, *Venus and Adonis* and *Lucrece*. It is true that the history plays carry far fewer references to Ovid than the comedies or tragedies, but the bodies both on stage and in the dialogue of these plays are no less metamorphic and fragmented. Jonathan Bate sees elements of Ovid, for example, in Prince Hal's self-proclaimed metamorphosis, especially as that change is figured in Vernon's description of the transformed prince 'into a feathered Mercury upon a fiery Pegasus'. However, the principles of bodily fragmentation that extend right through the history plays go far beyond this kind of literary allusion or analogy.[9]

Another Ovidian reference in the history plays that Bate picks up on is Richard II's comparison of himself to 'glistering Phaëton' as he descends from the walls of Flint Castle, abasing himself before the victorious Bolingbroke. Bate reads this phrase allegorically, as an image through which the fractious politics of the late 1590s can be refracted, discussed and obfuscated. If it is an allegory, then it is not so in the analogical sense meant by Bate but, rather, in the Benjaminian baroque sense of allegory: not straightforward analogy but a figure that contains traces of its own ruin. The Richard/Phaëton figure stands in either for Elizabeth (no longer able to control her courtiers) or for Essex and other ambitious courtiers (bound to fall as the result of their overweening ambition). When Richard, during the course of this scene, imagines himself as so debased that he is buried at a crossroads to have his head walked over by every passing subject ('Some way of common trade, where subjects' feet / May hourly trample on their sovereign head'), this topsy-turvy world does seem to invite Bate's allegorical reading. But by the time Richard's speech is in full flight, his verbal dexterity starts to describe bodily relations that are much harder to pin down in any straightforward way. He mockingly claims that Bolingbroke ought no longer to kneel to him:

> Fair cousin, you debase your princely knee
> To make the base earth proud with kissing it.
> Me rather had my heart might feel your love
> Than my unpleased eye see your courtesy.
> Up cousin, up. Your heart is up, I know,
> Thus high at least, although your knee be low. (3.3.188–93)

Richard insists that Bolingbroke ought not to feign a subservience that he surely does not intend, and this provides the scene with a critical and satirical range that extends beyond the local references argued by Bate. But in the midst of his speech, in a manner typical of Richard's dialogue, the metaphors run away from him. The 'knee' at the end of the speech is the same 'princely knee' at the start of the speech; this seems to make obvious Richard's intention to slight Bolingbroke. But we also have hearts and eyes, kisses and feelings; the coherence of bodily relations starts to unravel. Richard is not quite able to grasp how to articulate the language of this fragmented body. When, in the next speech, he addresses his uncle, York, and says to him, 'give me your hands' and 'dry your eyes', the proliferation of body parts continues. The ostensible meanings are, perhaps, clear; he is trying to think through what this loss of loyal affection means for his kingship. But the effect of the speech is one in which the dialogue starts to become disarticulated from the performing bodies on stage. His speeches sound like blazon, but it is a blazon that does not well describe the bodies on stage, or their actions.

Similarly, in two scenes that seem most to isolate Richard on stage, the image of his sovereign isolation unravels from the body of the king. These two scenes are his arrival on a Welsh beach on his return from Ireland and his later imprisonment. In this chapter, I first consider Richard II's solitude, primarily in the beach scene and by means of Derrida's concept of sovereign ipseity. I then conclude by analysing the transactions of Richard's deposition and imprisonment as moments in which sustainable theories of sovereignty are challenged.

## Richard II as Robinson Crusoe

In the second year of a series of lectures, published under the title *The Beast and the Sovereign*, Derrida pays particular attention to ideas of isolation, solitude and what he calls the '*ipseity*' (solipsistic self-sameness) of sovereignty. Discussing Jean-Jacques Rousseau's reading of Daniel Defoe's *Robinson Crusoe*, he detects what he calls a fantasy of 'pre-political' solitude that is shared by the two eighteenth-century writers. This shared fantasy is a version of sovereign will that imagines itself as something isolated, insular and self-contained: a marooned body on an island state. Rousseau, Derrida argues, thinks of Crusoe as Adam-like and Adam as 'sovereign of the world like Robinson of his island'.[10] Derrida glosses this Adamic Crusoe as a version of 'absolute political sovereignty'. However, the idea that this solitary figure might be thought of as truly 'political' is only ever fantastical, insulated as he is from other people or other things: 'this sovereignty which is absolute because it is pre-political, the hyperbolical, pre-political or ultra-political sovereignty that is the prize of solitude or isolation, of loneliness or of absolute insularity …'[11]

'Hyper', 'pre' and 'ultra': beyond and before; absolutism is always an untimely fantasy, a form of 'political' power that cannot be realised in the here and now. The only way that sovereignty could ever be 'absolute', Derrida suggests, is if it is somehow protected from any actual political engagement. And, in Defoe's novel, this insular/island solitude does not – cannot – last. Derrida selects as his critical moment the time when, left to his own devices, Crusoe invents a machine for himself. This moment, for Derrida, is the occasion when Crusoe's dreams of self-sufficiency collapse. Through making this decision, the putatively self-sufficient sovereign places his relationships with the world on a different footing. The machine that he makes is a wheel for sharpening a knife that he has brought with him on to the island from the shipwrecked boat. In arming himself in this way, Crusoe now enters the political world proper, as distinct from the mere fantasies of sovereignty that he harbours in his 'pre-political' solitude. Crusoe, Derrida tells us, compares this act to 'a major political exploit':

> And when I say *major*, I mean sovereign, majestic, i.e. *grand* with that *majestas* that in Latin meant sovereignty. I believe there are good reasons to think that this political analogy is neither insignificant nor fortuitous. We are indeed talking about an act of sovereignty and a question of life or death when a living being invents all alone, by himself, a technique, a machine designed to ensure his survival, to decide as to his life and his death, to avoid being swallowed alive.[12]

Crusoe may invent his new machine 'all alone', but the invention assumes the existence of other people. In the movement between these two passages (the earlier passage in which Derrida considers the 'pre-political' nature of Crusoe's supposed solitude and this passage in which he describes a sovereign 'act'), Derrida implies that the island fantasy of a 'pre-political' self-sovereignty is abandoned in Crusoe's reorientation to the world through a weapon. It is an '*act* of sovereignty' rather than an image or idea of sovereignty. In this act, he shares characteristics with other Defoe characters, as described by Srinivas Aravamudan when he calls them 'Mini-sovereigns', 'making law through a founding violence'.[13] Crusoe's island is not 'intire of it selfe' after all, but 'a part of the maine'.[14] The implication is that sovereignty cannot be contained within the isolated figure of a solitary man's body but is, rather, made manifest through engagements with the world.[15] Images of early modern sovereignty might tend towards an absolute solitude but this isolation cannot sustain sovereign power. In *Robinson Crusoe*, the apprehension of danger from potential opponents is what initiates this new version of what it now means to be sovereign. This is a different kind of sovereignty that might not even *be* sovereignty proper: an assemblage of the organic and the machine, something that elsewhere in these lectures Derrida refers to as 'prosthstatics'.[16] It turns out that Crusoe could never have been self-sufficient but that he needed both an object through which to work his will upon the world and, also, an opponent or a subject upon which to practise his sovereign authority. Footsteps appear on the beach.

J. Hillis Miller reads Derrida's understanding of solitude *vis-à-vis* the politics of sovereignty differently, preferring to highlight what he calls Derrida's 'unusual' insistence on 'inescapable solitude'. Tracing Derrida's rescription of Heideggerian ontology in relation to the idea of community, Miller quotes Derrida: 'There is no world, there are only islands.'[17] What motivates a different emphasis on my part, one that leans rather more on the precarity of sovereignty's supposed solitude and the porosity of the state of being 'enisled', is that I am not, as I think Miller is, assuming an ontology that could ever be entirely separated from a politics of sovereignty. That is, Miller imagines that there might be a way of being in the world that does not assume a politics of sovereignty; I do not think that this is possible. If, to follow Miller's reading of Derrida, we are all inevitably Robinson Crusoes – 'enisled' as Miller calls it – then as soon as claims to sovereignty are made by one of these 'enisled' figures, this supposed solitude is no longer sustainable. Miller is circumspect about his own reading, admitting at one point that it 'goes against what one might assume Derrida believed'.[18] Miller is right that Derrida, compared to Jean-Luc Nancy for example, does not confirm the prior existence of community, anterior to and preceding singular identity. So, unlike Nancy, Derrida does not affirm 'that the world has no other origin than [a] singular multiplicity of origins'.[19] However, in a double movement characteristic of deconstruction, any Derridean dissolution of community is not quite the same thing as a secure basis for a self-similitude that can, then, be used to underwrite a sovereign authority as it might be localised in a singular figure. If, in Derrida, community is revealed as 'always constructed and therefore, deconstructible', this is equally true of the apparently self-identical isolation of the sovereign.[20] As Derrida writes elsewhere, 'wherever we think we are up against the problems of sovereignty . . . the question is not that of sovereignty or nonsovereignty but that of the modalities of transfer and division of a sovereignty said to be indivisible – *said and supposed to be indivisible but always divisible*'.[21]

It is in this movement between a 'supposed' indivisibility and actual divisibility that questions are posed about sovereignty in Shakespeare's history plays, perhaps especially in *Richard II*. Shakespeare's Richard II is a Robinson Crusoe figure, ahead of his time.[22] Like Derrida's version of Crusoe, he gathers to himself fantasies of what might be thought of as a 'pre-political' isolation (supposed indivisible) and, like Crusoe, he does this on a beach, on the fringes of an island over which he assumes, or imagines, he holds sovereign power. In these untenable fantasies, he sometimes seems to think that his sovereign will is completely coterminous with the way that the world is ordered, a world that he fantasises as remaining undisturbed by the footsteps of any intruder. But, just as Crusoe's island solitude is inevitably disrupted, so Richard's isolation is not substantiated in the action or dialogue of the play. Footsteps always arrive on the beach. If it's not Friday, it's Bolingbroke. As Greg Dening writes in a different context, 'A beach is always marked by the footsteps in the sand of the befores, the wet soaking edginess of the now, and the vague future.'[23] As he returns to the Welsh beach from his Irish exploits, Richard would like the beach to be a nice, clean sheet with no prior footsteps, but this is never the case.

In *Richard II*, John of Gaunt's 'sceptred isle' speech ensures that he has been the character most often associated with the idealised metaphor of the island kingdom. But Richard, too, entertains and extends Gaunt's delusion that England and its monarchy can be insulated from the world in this way. In Gaunt's famous speech, he advocates for the land of England as a foil for the solitary jewel of an imaginary monarchy, protected from the incursions of enemies, both within and without. But he also describes the current reality of Richard's reign as an auto-immune kingdom that has destroyed itself from within, that 'Hath made a shameful conquest of itself' (2.1.66). Virgil's first *Eclogue* is the most prominent literary source for Gaunt's images of insular geography. In this source, 'Britannos' is described as a place that is well beyond the collapsing world of imperial Rome, even perhaps outside of politics: 'ultra-political'. It might be a place of harsh exile for the Roman soldiers who are sent there, but at least it is at a safe distance from the Roman countryside that has been turned upside down by civil and foreign conflict. However, in the latter days of Ricardian and/or Elizabethan England, 'Britannos' is itself on the brink of becoming a world turned in on itself in the same way. Virgil's exhausted pastoral, intersected by political boundaries (home/abroad, town/country, what's mine/what's yours), has now come to define the formerly 'pre-political' isolation of Britain as a 'tenant farm' bound by 'rotten parchment bonds'.

Just like Gaunt, Richard also struggles to imagine England/'Britannos' as an insular kingdom, and his version of the island also becomes self-destructive. That he is arriving from Ireland already gives the lie to any specious unity on the part of an English claim to splendid isolation. Returning to the shorelines of his island realm from that other island, Ireland, he prays for a land that is unconditionally an extension of his sovereign will:

Feed not thy sovereign's foe, my gentle earth,
Nor with thy sweets comfort his ravenous sense,

> But let thy spiders that suck up thy venom
> And heavy-gaited toads lie in their way,
> Doing annoyance to the treacherous feet
> Which with usurping steps do trample thee.
> Yield stinging nettles to mine enemies;
> And when they from thy bosom pluck a flower,
> Guard it I pray thee with a lurking adder
> Whose double tongue may with a mortal touch
> Throw death upon thy sovereign's enemies. (3.2.12–22)

This is in the form of an incantation, and Richard's spell attempts to conjure into being a realm in which – just as for Rousseau's Adamic Crusoe – no distinction is made between his will and the ordering of the island; Richard dreams up an imaginary absolutist monarchy that has everything within its purview: not just people, but animals (spiders, adders and toads), vegetables (nettles and flowers) and minerals (the 'gentle earth' itself).

However, even here, at the very moment when Richard is desperately seeking to assert his exceptional status as a sovereign, his idea of sovereign rule remains dependent on the proximity of other things, on multiple relationships to other things: other creatures, other people, spiders, toads, earth etc. For all that Richard is trying, in this speech, to immunise himself against outside influence, he is in the organic world that Jeffrey Cohen has described as 'potentially indifferent to humanity and yet ... intimately continuous with us'.[24] Richard's earth has its excrescences – its 'sweets' – for which Richard is unable fully to account.[25]

This imaginary world in which he thinks that his sovereign will might have some effect is a place that closely – if unexpectedly – resembles the teeming, cloyingly fecund fairy-world of *A Midsummer Night's Dream*, a play that is roughly contemporary with *Richard II*. In *A Midsummer Night's Dream*, the principles of metamorphic change operate at a microscopic level through the magical properties of forest flora and fauna. Robert Watson describes the world of *Midsummer* as representative of a widespread early modern awareness that human will can never be confined within the solitary person:

> Shakespeare's characters are never insular nor unitary – not only because they are threads in a dramatic fabric rather than actual persons, but also because actual persons are neither insular nor unitary. Elizabethan culture understood human beings as often occupied by forces meaningfully alien to their conscious personal will.[26]

Richard's intention, on his arrival back into his kingdom, is to exorcise those alien occupying forces and to invoke a mystical sovereign power over lands and creatures that he tries to insist would be an extension of his will. Inalienable or absolute sovereignty is, then, one name for an untenable fantasy that we can ever be wholly unoccupied by 'forces alien to [our] personal will'. The effect of Richard's speech on the beach is to reveal an island that is already swarming with forms of life that could hardly be within Richard's control. His list gets away from him, and the 'sweets' that he calls upon ultimately indicate a nature that exceeds his purview. Towards the end of his career, Shakespeare, in *The Tempest*, revisits the idea of sovereign will in the context of a contest over prior ownership of an island. By that point, his magician-king Prospero is, to a much greater extent, in a position to make the kinds of demands that Richard makes: that the stones, plants and animals of the island obey his will and assist him in re-establishing his position on the throne. But even Prospero is forced to contend with the realisation that his is a double fantasy: that his magic is just another illusion that can readily be broken, and that the island was already occupied before he got there.

In this speech, Richard uses the allegorising logic of the micro- and macrocosm. As a rhetorical strategy and as an aspect of analogical thinking, this is something that frequently sustains images of divinely appointed monarchy, in which, for example, God's rule is taken as a model for the rule of the monarch. But Richard's excessively alive kingdom, even though it is imagined through relations of scale, is one that is crawling with animate beings that outstrip any single jurisdiction. More even than the archbishop's beehive in *Henry V*, this is a 'busy' world. Moreover, what enables Richard's fantasy of absolute rule, what provokes and sustains it, is the dream's imminent and inevitable destruction. Without the enmity of the 'usurping steps' – the inevitable footsteps on the beach – there would be no delusional response from Richard. Even as he fantasises a self-sufficient, but utterly unstable, sovereign autonomy, the impetus for this impossible dream is the always-approaching tread, the steps that were always approaching, the intruder walking on an island which is, after all, not his. Richard calls it '*my* gentle earth' but it is emphatically not *his*, any more than Prospero's island unequivocally belongs to him. Prospero will have his Caliban, but Richard already has his Bolingbroke.

The 'adder' in Richard's speech – the 'double adder' that 'may with a mortal touch / Throw death upon thy sovereign's enemies' – is an instantly recognisable, if slightly skewed, reference to the breach of Eden's security by Satan and to the arrival of death into paradise. In Richard's imaginary island realm, he tries to harness this agent of death as a weapon of his own. The adder, however, has a 'double tongue', and Richard is forced to confront, and then retreat from, thoughts of death. In response to this, he goes on to dream up new island realms for himself, but these are now vastly reduced from the extensive, world-dominating fantasies that he entertained a moment ago. Now the island is confined first to his body, a 'model', he says, 'of the barren earth' and, then, from the 'paste and cover' of his body, Richard's island world is further confined to his own fragile skull:

> Our lands, our lives and all are Bolingbroke's,
> And nothing can we call our own but death
> And that small model of the barren earth
> Which serves as paste and cover to our bones.
> ... For within the hollow crown
> That rounds the mortal temples of a king
> Keeps Death his court; (3.2.151–4, 160–2)

The 'gentle earth' of his previous invocation has now become the 'barren earth' of his own body or skull. At first, Death belongs to him; it is, apparently, the only thing that he *can* call 'our own'. But then Death sets up an independent court of *his* own within Richard's head, a head which is modelled upon the earth while also, itself, being sculpted from 'paste'. The primary meaning of this odd simile – earth figured as 'paste' – is to compare the crust of the earth and, hence, Richard's skull, to brittle pastry: his body as a kind of pie. The idealising and analogising tendencies of micro- and macrocosmic thought are always being undone in the language of *Richard II* as categories bleed into one another: body-becoming-earth-becoming-pastry. 'Earth' and 'paste': are they really metaphors? Not quite. Are they literal? Again, not quite. Rather, like the fairy landscape of Richard's earlier speech, these are *topoi* wherein ideal figurations of sovereignty *might* be constructed but where they are, instead, revealed as illusory. Richard's bodily metaphors for sovereignty are founded in a materiality that is paradoxically both obdurate and indefinable and, in the self-cancelling complexities of Richard's figurative language, figurations of sovereignty defy stable identification.

### 'Is not the king's name forty thousand names': Disorderly Pronouns in *Richard II*

This scene in which Richard returns to the Welsh coast too late, and to a kingdom that has already broken apart, is a major turning point in the narrative of his downfall. The scene is also critically concerned with the extent and limitations – the administration – of his sovereign power. That is, while Richard dreams of what it might be like to *be* sovereign, he is necessarily engaged, however incompetently and reluctantly, in the business of *enacting*, or even administering, sovereignty. Harry Berger Jr suggests that Richard's weakness or ineptitude might better be read as a deliberate political strategy, in which his 'self-pity' is a means by which he tries to regain lost agency:

> After returning from Ireland he refuses to take action and instead flaunts his helplessness and luxuriates in self-pity. But since we know that he is a knowing accomplice in his undoing even as he loudly proclaims himself an innocent victim, we have a hard time taking his self-representation as a betrayed Christ-figure at face value.[27]

Richard-as-Christ has been taken to heart, or too literally, too often, perhaps through the pervasive influence of Ernst Kantorowicz's reading of the play in *The King's Two Bodies*. In distinction from that tradition of interpreting Richard, Berger argues that the rather static image of Richard as an avatar of a metaphysically grounded royal power is put under pressure if we consider what actually happens in the play. That is, Richard's actions are no match for the image of the king, and of sovereignty, that sometimes inheres in the play's sacrificial language. I am less sanguine about ascribing this contradiction to Richard's own political agency, as much as to a distinction that seems always to pertain between stasis and action, or between apotheosis and materialisation, that adheres to most considerations of early modern sovereignty. This is what I meant earlier when, in discussing J. Hillis Miller's responses to Derrida's thoughts on sovereignty, I made a distinction between an ontology and a politics of sovereignty. What might be found on, or in, the island realm of Richard's imaginings disturbs any capacity that he might have to sustain his dreams of being absolutely sovereign. Richard realises that imagining an island realm (or realms if we include Ireland) as a kingdom of his own is not only fantastical; it is even idiotic and contemptible. He imagines Death as a *danse macabre* 'antic' who allows him, only briefly, 'to monarchize':

> Infusing him with self and vain conceit,
> As if this flesh which walls about our life
> Were brass impregnable; and humoured thus
> Comes at the last, and with a little pin
> Bores through his castle wall; and farewell, king! (3.2.162–6)

Richard's subjunctive mood ('As if this . . . were') articulates the provisional nature of the island realm as already on the brink of invasion from within, an auto-immune sovereignty that contains, in the alliances that it makes with death, the beginnings of its end.

But as well as Richard's tortured dialogue, the stage itself plays a part in holding his fantasies of unified and unifying sovereignty to some account. The wooden boards of The Theatre (where the play was likely first staged in 1595) might briefly be imagined as an island in Richard's dialogue. Ralph Berry describes how this might work with the equally solitary Richard of Gloucester in *Henry VI* part two. The future Richard III dreams of grasping the crown, and stands on a stage that has become a geographical promontory: 'Like one that stands upon a promontory / And spies a far-off shore where he would tread, /... / And chides the sea that sunders him from thence' (3.2.134–8). In this scene, as Berry sees it, the stage becomes a metonym for the island nation:

> That [promontory] is not a bad description of the stage, thrusting in upon the audience. But observe the clarity and firmness of Shakespeare's composite image. The solitary actor, well downstage, is the man on the promontory. The audience is the sea. Richard, looking beyond the humanity from whom he is sundered, fastens his gaze upon some distant prospect that he will never attain. It is all there, in the starkness and resonance of the central image.[28]

The whole of the scene in which Richard II returns from Ireland echoes this resonant image from the earlier play: a king on the borders of his kingdom searching for some means to become synonymous with it. However, there are always the exits and entrances on to – and off – the stage that work to undo this fantasy even before it starts. In imagining his actions as ironic performance (the scornful 'monarchize' implies a lack of real capacity) and his own body as a building that can be penetrated, this always-about-to-be-invaded stage/island emerges as a figure of insular sovereignty in the process of being undone. The stage is never isolated; characters come and go. Donna Hamilton reads into this scene a breakdown of Richard's bodily integrity, comparing its imagery to that found in the work of John Fortescue, a mid-fifteenth-century judge who insists on the mutual 'life blood' that is needed in 'byndyng' together king, subjects and the law.[29] The corollary of this is that, left alone, the body of the king withers and dies. Richard's paradox of a castle wall that is so fragile that it can be penetrated by a pin is, then, expressively emblematic of the precarious nature of the king's body as imaginary locus of sovereign power.

In conjunction with this deployment of the stage-space as precarious sovereign state, Richard's dialogue succeeds in unravelling his sovereign position through an extremely erratic use of pronouns. Throughout the play, Richard alternates between using the first person singular, the royal plural 'we', and talking about himself in the third person. In this scene, this is most strikingly exemplified in the astonishingly inarticulate response he makes when Aumerle tries to get him to pull himself together. Aumerle entreats him, 'Comfort, my liege. Remember who you are', and Richard responds:

> I had forgot myself. Am I not king?
> Awake, thou sluggard majesty, thou sleep'st!
> Is not the king's name forty thousand names?
> Arm, arm, my name! A puny subject strikes
> At thy great glory. Look not to the ground,
> Ye favourites of a king: are we not high?
> High be our thoughts. (3.2.79–85)

To use a rather tired pun, Richard does not at all 're-member' himself in the way that Aumerle is looking for. Richard's inarticulacy emerges in the way that his speech fails to fasten itself on to a secure set of relations between his body and those of other people. In quick succession, he refers to himself (and himself as king) with several different pronouns. He starts with an 'I' but then follows this by questioning the referent of that 'I': 'Am I not king?' This is followed in turn by referring to aspects of himself as 'thou', 'the king's name', 'thy great glory' and then 'we'. Richard switches confusedly between first, second and third person and between singular and plural. This muddling of pronouns – evident in Richard's dialogue throughout the play – is compounded by the multiplication of the 'king's name' into 'forty thousand names' and the use of the second person to address different things and people, as well as himself. In apostrophe, it is used for his own cowardly inertia ('thou sluggard majesty') but then 'my name' switches to the second person as 'thy great glory'. But then, presumably, it is his onstage audience of attendants who are addressed as '*Ye* favourites of a king'. Faced with the prospect of encountering an enemy, Richard's use of pronouns seems unable to restrict itself to the first person, singular or plural. Rather, his identity travels through different configurations of personhood; this is not just the royal 'we' but a royal multitude, some members of which are not integral to his own person. Again, the sustaining fiction of the royal 'we' which might work to fix sovereignty in both the temporal body of a particular king and the eternal body of kingship in general is not available here. Pronouns multiply and contradict each other in the various ways that Richard attempts to orient himself towards other people, and to the world. Charles Forker sees Richard, in this scene, as 'ritualis[ing] the abandonment of his sacred body, the body symbolised by his throne'.[30] But the binarism implied by this division between sacred and profane bodies is not adequate to the ever-increasing multiplicities of personhood that are a feature of the dialogue of *Richard II*. Derrida's 'modalities of transfer and division' are, here, realised and confounded through Richard's confusion of pronouns.

In dramatic dialogue, pronouns are important in very particular ways. Staged dialogue rapidly becomes incomprehensible if pronouns are not clearly anchored to specific people; pronouns are exactly what establishes relationships between differentiated characters, between characters and objects, and between characters and abstract ideas. Their coherent use is essential if the words that actors speak are to be tied firmly to specific circumstances. Their function, in dramatic dialogue, is primarily deictic, requiring a specific referent and firming up a sense of the play's world, locating specific people in specific places, with specific relationships to each other. As Keir Elam notes, they are one of 'the primary means whereby language gears itself to the speaker and receiver . . . as well as to the supposed physical environment at large and to the objects that fill it'.[31] For Richard to muddle his pronouns in the way that he does means that his dialogue is always on the brink of becoming meaningless. The integrity of the individual body on stage is usually consolidated, produced even, by an accurate and consistent use of pronouns; we know who somebody is in relation to somebody else because of how each of them uses 'I', 'we' or 'you'. Dialogue becomes anchored to personation through a consistency of usage and, in turn, those characters become meaningful within the space of the stage. But in Richard's speeches, that clarity is constantly, and often radically, put at risk. At stake is his status as a coherent person that would connect the actor to the role and, in turn, to dialogue and to stage-space. If the tenor of this particular speech is a reaffirmation of strong kingship ('Are we not high?'), its effect – through this pronominal confusion and consequent disintegration of his person – is the opposite. At the very moment that Richard recollects his capacities as king in the face of armed rebellion, his performance of sovereignty is dissipated through his incapacity to maintain well-defined relationships between himself, his role as king, his subjects and the material world that constitutes his realm.

That Richard's identity disintegrates during the course of this play is hardly a new observation, but the nature of the disintegration has sometimes been missed by those too willing to read into it a straightforward restatement of the doctrine of the 'king's two bodies'. If we were to follow the influential reading of *Richard II* offered by Kantorowicz in *The King's Two Bodies*, this kind of psychic and linguistic breakdown on Richard's part (where he seems incapable of distinguishing one person from another, himself from his role, or his role from his dependents) would be taken to signal a crack appearing precisely along the rift that divides the worldly person of the king from the eternal perpetuation of the monarchy. Through the play's debate around whether Richard can disavow his worldly crown, then, the dualistic metaphysics of sovereignty – originating with god but located in the body of the king – are revealed. The bifurcated view of kingship that presents itself in Kantorowicz is picked up everywhere in criticism that attends to Shakespeare's history plays, particularly *Richard II*. But the body parts of Shakespeare's history plays are always more various and more multiple than Kantorowiczian dualities might allow. Richard's sovereignty comprises more than two bodies; this multiplicity is realised on stage during the scene of his murder in prison.

## Richard in Prison: Against Political Theology

It would be wrong to suggest that the binary divisions that are important to Kantorowicz (man/God, Judas/Jesus, temporal/eternal etc.) are not at all at work in *Richard II*; they surely are. But the ruptures that transect Richard's personhood as king, and as a potential repository for sovereignty, are many times more multiple than might be suggested by a reliance on those binaries alone. What Kantorowicz calls the 'oneness of the double body' is never really there in *Richard II*.[32] Even though Shakespeare is working within a world where this kind of political theology determines some of the forms and figures within which he and his characters are caught, the way that sovereignty (the pre-eminent capacity to construct the world) works in Shakespeare's plays is much more transactional, and much less stable, than this suggests. That is, sovereignty might sometimes be conceived as having an origin in some relation to Christ's passion and, in turn, this must have some impact on the way in which the bodies of the king and his subjects are represented. But, as I have been suggesting and as this book illustrates throughout, this understanding far from exhausts the many more multiple ways in which bodies interact in the production of sovereignty in these plays.

Deborah Shuger, investigating the presence of political theology in Shakespeare's Jacobean play *Measure for Measure*, makes the point that the dominant political language of early modern Europe was, notwithstanding her own interests in relation to *Measure*, usually more secular than theological, more Aristotelian than Pauline. Early modern political thought was, Shuger writes, concerned primarily with 'the allocation and management of power', 'its distribution, transfer, acquisition, administration, and loss'.[33] If, as Shuger argues, in the particular circumstances of the early years of James I's reign, Shakespeare investigates the workings of a state that starts to diverge from this and to look a bit more like a political theology, deriving sovereignty from Christological conceptions of transcendence, then in the history plays from the 1590s we are much more in the Aristotelian world of 'allocation and management', or what I have already quoted Derrida as calling 'the modalities of transfer and division of a sovereignty said to be indivisible'.[34] That is, sovereignty is shown, in these plays, not to inhere in any one body, even if that one body is occasionally conceived of as the mystically divided and conjoined 'king's two bodies'. Rather, sovereignty is made manifest through more variable and unpredictable engagements with the world, including the organic with the mechanical, the 'natural' with the 'artificial'.

Anselm Haverkamp argues something similar in relation to Kantorowicz's reading of *Richard II*. He contends that, while Kantorowicz is happy to follow Shakespeare's lead in seeing Richard as an adherent of the legal fiction of the king's two bodies, the play as a whole does more than simply unravel Richard's ownership of those two bodies. Rather, it underwrites the emergence of the principle, within English law, of the crown's subjection to legal process. As he writes, the crown is not simply above the law but 'under the law above the law'.[35] In this, Haverkamp is following Lorna Hutson in arguing that if the introduction of the 'two bodies' thesis into Elizabethan legal discourse has any effect at all, it is precisely the opposite effect from instantiating a metaphysically extra-legal status for the monarchy.[36] Rather, it places the acts of the monarch within the jurisdiction of English law. The office of the monarchy is separated from the body of the king, or queen, precisely in order to produce a legal entity that is appropriately answerable to the law and that can be understood as such when it is beneficial to the overriding good of the commonwealth. Hutson argues that the introduction of the two bodies metaphor into Elizabethan legal discourse in the commentaries of Edmund Plowden (so influential in Kantorowicz) is not at all a concerted attempt to locate the state in the isolated, mystical body of the monarch. Rather, it forms just one part of his project to reconcile English common law with statute law, and whose effect 'marginalises, rather than makes central, the symbolic power of the monarch'.[37]

Behind both Haverkamp's and Hutson's critique of Kantorowicz's deployment of political theology is, also, a repudiation of Schmitt's influential theory of sovereignty as political theology, a theory that excludes the sovereign from the law by means of a capacity to make extra-legal decisions: 'Sovereign is he who decides the exception' is Schmitt's famous – now infamous – definition.[38] This critique is explicit in Haverkamp, and implicit in the arguments put forward by Hutson.

Haverkamp invokes Agamben's critical readings of Schmitt as a way to air his own disagreements. And, as suggested in the Introduction, Agamben's work has revived interest in Schmittian political theology, developing his own theories of sovereignty that lie both within, and in opposition to, the strain of thought introduced by Schmitt's concept of the sovereign exception.[39] As Haverkamp writes, 'Agamben's *Homo Sacer* confronts and refutes Schmitt's mythic superstructure of the exception with its proto-typical application in Roman law.'[40] In Agamben, this inaugurating instance of the sovereign exception also produces a corollary for the extra-legal position of the sovereign in an utterly abject body that is vulnerable to violent death but that, like the sovereign, is outside the law: *homo sacer*. But if it is the case that Richard's persona as king unravels during the course of the play, it is not the case that this *only* serves to lay bare the workings of a political theology, as arguments derived from Kantorowicz – whether in Schmitt or in Agamben – would have it. In order to pursue this, I want to follow Richard's production of insular kingdoms into the cramped space of his prison cell.

The prison scene where Richard plays 'in one person many people' (5.5.31) repeats and intensifies the tropes of his earlier arrival on the Welsh coastline from Ireland. Here, too, his world-making fantasies, through which he populates the empty dungeon, are haunted by immanent destruction coming both from within Richard himself and from the doors leading on and offstage, into and out of his prison cell. The cell replaces the island or the Welsh coastline as the emblematic space of his solitude. But, as before, this solitude is unsustainable.[41] Frequently identified, in critical accounts and particularly in performances, as a figure of exemplary pathos, what is not so often recognised is that, in this final scene, Richard is, in fact, all action. This scene shows him to be, of all Shakespeare's kings, the one most personally capable of violent combat. He is far from the passive figure of tragic pathos that he is sometimes taken to be, and for which his soliloquies may have prepared us. When it comes to it, Richard stands up and fights.[42] As his enemies arrive on stage in the persons of Exton and his four servants, Richard turns to the sword, killing two of these invaders of his island/cell/kingdom/stage:

> How now! What means death in this rude assault?
>   [*He seizes a weapon from a man, and kills him.*]
> Villain, thy own hand yields thy death's instrument.
> Go thou, and fill another room in hell!
>   *Here Exton strikes him down.*
> That hand shall burn in never-quenching fire
> That staggers thus my person. Exton, thy fierce hand
> Hath with the King's blood stained the King's own land.

Mount, mount, my soul; thy seat is up on high,
Whilst my gross flesh sinks downward here to die.
   [*He dies.*] (5.5.105–12)⁴³

As in the earlier scene, Richard speaks in the first, second and third persons when talking about himself. Or, rather, as he talks about *parts* of himself as they fall away from each other. The apprehension that he has of his soul's ascension to heaven at the close of the scene might seem to replicate the doctrine of the king's two bodies as expounded by Kantorowicz. In some ways, it is its most perfect articulation in the whole play, more so even than the mirror scene during the abdication. But the apparently perfect stasis of this Kantorowiczian metaphor is challenged by the agitated action of the scene, by the rapid and confused turn to weapons, and by the frenzied exchange of death-dealing blows. This is not an apotheosis; it is a bloodbath. Unlike the abdication scene, in which Richard might challenge Bolingbroke's right to sever his body from the sacred body of kingship but which, in terms of action, performs a relatively ritualistic transfer of power, this scene is violent and chaotic. The dominant body parts at this stage are not the 'rounded temples' of the sovereign-king, isolated in elegant pathos, but, rather, the multiple and bloodied 'hands' of assassins and victim. The word 'hand' is repeated three times, and is also lent emphasis, highlighted through being the first rhyming word in this part of the dialogue (tellingly, perhaps, with 'land', given the nature of many of the complaints against Richard's mishandling of the kingship). More importantly, the hand is foregrounded in the onstage action that is demanded by the dialogue: a frantic bout of hand-to-hand combat. The 'hand', as shall be seen in Chapter 3 of this book, has a critical relationship both to agency and to sovereign will in Shakespeare's history plays. It is also the last word spoken in *Richard II*, as Henry IV acknowledges his own 'guilty hand'. Here, the scene of Richard's death is not the beautiful tableau that Richard, himself, attempts to bring into view ('Mount, mount, my soul!') but a bloodstained mess of violence – a stage littered with three corpses – wherein it is difficult to see who it is that kills whom.

If we too willingly accept the idea of Richard as Christ-like martyr and, through this, an idea of sacral majesty that underpins an absolutist sovereignty, then we are accepting Richard's delusions rather than what we have seen actually happen on stage, and what Richard has actually done. Exton closes the scene:

This dead King to the living King I'll bear.
Take hence the rest, and give them burial here. (5.5.117–18)

His words, while potentially referencing the ritual form of the 'king's two bodies' ('dead King', 'living King', 'The King is dead; long live the King') end up, instead, pointing towards what he calls the 'rest': the bloody remains of the dead who are cluttering up the scene and who, confusingly, are both to be taken 'hence' and also buried 'here', on stage. The decorous rhyming couplets with which this scene closes (not just Exton's last two lines but from Richard's final speech onwards) attempt to re-envisage the charnel house that the stage has become as a scene of monarchical apotheosis. But they are not successful. The 'rest' have to be lugged off stage. Whatever metaphysics are imagined in the transfer of sovereignty at this point ('dead King' becoming 'living King'), the stage upon which this takes place remains a bloody mess, the result of hands and weapons that are inescapably entangled with each other.

Even with his dying words, Richard tries to promote a new version of 'majesty' that is self-sustaining, underwritten by messianic pretensions. But what the picture of Richard's final moments on stage reveals, instead, is the multiform sovereignty of the 'prosthstatic' state. This is typical of Shakespeare's representations of sovereignty which, in their gruelling reproduction of the mechanics of sovereign power, reveal sovereign bodies that are disarticulated rather than integrated, multiple and multiform rather than solitary and unique. In the next chapter, an obsession with necks and throats in the dialogue of *Henry V* reveals similarly disarticulated forms of sovereignty, this time through versions of inadequate translation and substitution.

## Notes

1. Jean-Jacques Rousseau, *The Social Contract*, trans. Maurice Cranston (Harmondsworth: Penguin, 1968), pp. 70–1.
2. Shannon, *Sovereign Amity*, p. 155.
3. Michael Harrawood, 'High-Stomached Lords: Imagination, Force, and the Body in Shakespeare's *Henry VI* Plays', *Journal for Early Modern Cultural Studies* 7.1 (2007), p. 90.
4. John Michael Archer, *Sovereignty and Intelligence: Spying and Court Culture in the English Renaissance* (Stanford: Stanford University Press, 1995), pp. 31–2.
5. Archer, *Sovereignty and Intelligence*, p. 38.
6. Harrawood, 'High-Stomached Lords', p. 93.
7. Lorenz, *The Tears of Sovereignty*, p. 23.
8. Lynn Enterline, *The Rhetoric of the Body from Ovid to Shakespeare* (Cambridge: Cambridge University Press, 2004), p. 1.
9. Jonathan Bate, *Shakespeare and Ovid* (Oxford: Oxford University Press, 1993), p. 125.

10. This is the translation of Rousseau that appears in the English version of Derrida's seminars. The original reads 'souverain du monde comme Robinson de son île', which is poorly translated in Maurice Cranston's English translation, an edition from which I will otherwise quote. He translates 'souverain du monde' as 'king of the world'. This is an error, given that Rousseau is taking great pains, at the beginning of *The Social Contract*, to situate the origins of sovereignty, not in the person of a 'king', but in the mutual acceptance of a contract. His 'souverain' here is laden with irony given that it comes just after a passage where he claims that he, too, might be the rightful sovereign of the world in that Rousseau himself must surely claim to be a descendant of Adam, or Noah, or of one of Noah's sons. Some of those ironies are carried over into Derrida's account of the two eighteenth-century writers.
11. Jacques Derrida, *The Beast and the Sovereign*, volume II, ed. Michel Lisse, Marie-Louise Mallet and Ginette Michaud, trans. Geoffrey Bennington (Chicago: University of Chicago Press, 2010), p. 21.
12. Derrida, *The Beast and the Sovereign*, vol. II, p. 82.
13. Srinivas Aravamudan, 'Subjects/Sovereigns/Rogues', *Eighteenth-Century Studies* 40.3 (2007), p. 461.
14. John Donne, *Devotions Upon Emergent Occasions*, ed. Anthony Raspa (Oxford: Oxford University Press, 1987), p. 87.
15. An influential reading of Defoe's politics in *Robinson Crusoe*, that of Manuel Schonhorn, would not agree with this idea of a self-sufficient sovereignty that is revealed as fantasy. Rather, Schonhorn sees Crusoe's claims to be sovereign of his island to be consistent with some of Defoe's own political beliefs, which run counter to contemporary Whiggish and Lockean contractualist versions of sovereignty. For Defoe, 'It is the warrior-king', Schonhorn writes, 'and not the community who is the soul animating the body politic' (Manuel Schonhorn, *Defoe's Politics: Parliament, Power, Kingship and* Robinson Crusoe (Cambridge: Cambridge University Press, 1991), p. 154). I have no doubt that there is a strand of this throughout *Robinson Crusoe*, but the narrative of the novel does not leave Crusoe's fantasies of self-originating sovereignty unchallenged. As soon as Crusoe has to deal with political issues more complex than his emblematic domination of Friday, he is obliged to enter into negotiations and, also, to transfer some of his authority to others. In particular, the English captain who Crusoe rescues from being marooned by his mutinous crew offers to cede his authority to Crusoe in a limited way in order to forward their joint political aims. We are told that the captain 'anticipated my [Crusoe's] proposals, by telling me that both he and the ship, if recovered, should be wholly directed and commanded by me in everything; and if the ship was not recovered, he would live and die with me in what part of the world soever I would send him' (Daniel Defoe, *Robinson Crusoe*, ed. John Richetti (Harmondsworth: Penguin, 2001), p. 253). So far, so absolutist. But then Crusoe returns with these conditions, 'That while you stay on this island with me, you will not pretend to any authority here; and if I put arms into your hands, you will upon all occasions give them up to me' (Defoe, *Robinson Crusoe*, p. 254). While this does accord with Schonhorn's sense of Crusoe as a 'warrior-king', there are also contractualist elements to what

is occurring here, and the narrative of *Robinson Crusoe*, as Crusoe moves further and further away from his solitude on the island, also reveals his ever-increasing dependence on the actions of others for his own safety. Furthermore, the whole novel traces Crusoe's return from the isolated world and sovereign state of the island to the economic interactions of the commercial world from which his sojourn on the island was a momentary (if lengthy) escape; this is an escapist fantasy of absolutism in the midst of a world of commercial uncertainty.

16. Jacques Derrida, *The Beast and the Sovereign*, volume I, ed. Michel Lisse, Marie-Louise Mallet and Ginette Michaud, trans. Geoffrey Bennington (Chicago: University of Chicago Press, 2009), *passim*.
17. J. Hillis Miller, 'Derrida Enisled', *Critical Inquiry* 33.2 (2007), p. 266. At stake in Miller's article is the distinction between Heidegger's '*Dasein*' (being there) and '*Mitsein*' (being with). Miller reads Derrida as unable to discern the possibility of *Mitsein*, ensuring that people are always 'radically impenetrable and secret' one to the other ('Derrida Enisled', p. 267). But if Derrida is sceptical of any prior claims for human 'community', he is equally sceptical of any claim that a person may be simply 'enisled', unique or singular.
18. Miller, 'Derrida Enisled', p. 266.
19. Jean-Luc Nancy, *Being-Singular-Plural*, trans. Robert D. Richardson and Anne E. O'Byrne (Stanford: Stanford University Press, 2000), p. 9.
20. Miller, 'Derrida Enisled', p. 268.
21. Derrida, *The Beast and the Sovereign*, vol. I, p. 291. My italics.
22. Crusoe, of course, if he is imagining himself as an absolutist monarch is, in the early eighteenth century, significantly behind the times.
23. Greg Dening, 'Performing on the Beaches of the Mind: An Essay', *History and Theory* 41.1 (2002), p. 18. Dening, in this article, is reviewing his career as a historian/beachcomber, tracing the marginal encounters that structure a certain history of the Pacific from his physical position on the Australian coast. While not a central concern of this book, the colonial implications of landing on a beach with the expectation that it bounds a land that is either unpeopled or is infinitely pliable to the will of the sovereign is not absent from what is going on here in Richard's rich fantasy life, and I will take it up in relation to *Richard III* in the final chapter.
24. Jeffrey Jerome Cohen, 'Stories of Stone', *post-medieval* 1.1/2 (2010), p. 58.
25. 'Sweets' is an interesting word for Shakespeare. Its multiple meanings most emerge in the Sonnets where it shifts between meaning something like goods or virtues ('Sweets with sweets war not', Sonnet 8) to carrying a close association with 'sweat' and with sin ('But that wild music burthens ever bough / And sweets grown common lose their dear delight', Sonnet 102).
26. Robert Watson, 'The Ecology of Self in *Midsummer Night's Dream*', in Lynne Bruckner and Dan Brayton (eds), *Ecocritical Shakespeare* (Burlington, VT: Ashgate, 2011), p. 52.
27. Harry Berger Jr, *Harrying: Skills of Offence in Shakespeare's* Henriad (New York: Fordham University Press, 2015), p. 26.
28. Ralph Berry, 'Metamorphoses of the Stage', *Shakespeare Quarterly* 33.1 (1982), pp. 9–10.

29. Donna Hamilton, 'The State of Law in *Richard II*', *Shakespeare Quarterly* 34.1 (1983), p. 10.
30. Charles R. Forker, 'Introduction', in William Shakespeare, *King Richard II*, ed. Charles R. Forker (London: Cengage, 2002), pp. 30–1.
31. Keir Elam, *The Semiotics of Theatre and Drama* (London: Routledge, 1980), p. 24.
32. Ernst Kantorowicz, *The King's Two Bodies* [1957] (Princeton: Princeton University Press, 1997), p. 31.
33. Deborah Shuger, *Political Theologies in Shakespeare's England: The Sacred and the State in* Measure for Measure (London: Palgrave, 2001), p. 41.
34. Derrida, *The Beast and the Sovereign*, vol. I, p. 291.
35. Anselm Haverkamp, '*Richard II*, Bracton, and the End of Political Theology', *Law and Literature* 16.3 (2004), p. 319.
36. Lorna Hutson, 'Not the King's Two Bodies: Reading the Body Politic in Shakespeare's *Henry IV* Plays', in Victoria Kahn and Lorna Hutson (eds), *Rhetoric and Law in Early Modern Europe* (New Haven: Yale University Press, 2001), pp. 166–89.
37. Hutson, 'Not the King's Two Bodies', p. 176.
38. Schmitt, *Political Theology*, p. 5.
39. Agamben, *Homo Sacer*; see also Giorgio Agamben, *State of Exception*, trans. Kevin Attell (Chicago: University of Chicago Press, 2005); Giorgio Agamben, *The Kingdom and the Glory: For a Theological Genealogy of Economy and Government*, trans. Lorenzo Chiesa (Stanford: Stanford University Press, 2011).
40. Haverkamp, '*Richard II*, Bracton, and the End of Political Theology', p. 321.
41. The third Arden editor, Charles Forker, cites Winifred Nowottny's reading of this speech in her book *The Language Poets Use* approvingly, and I agree. Nowottny writes, 'The whole speech ... is about Richard's experience of veering from one unstable rôle to another ... and his discovery in the process the sickening truth that all these rôles are unstable fabrications of his own mind, so that whether in or out of any particular rôle he is essentially nothing other than a consciousness which is simultaneously theatre and author'; Winifred Nowottny, *The Language Poets Use* (London: The Athlone Press, 1962), p. 89. Nowottny traces the simultaneous formation and dissolution of Richard's self-consciousness in this passage, in a manner that supports my own sense of the scene as articulating a version of sovereignty that is always 'veering' and 'unstable'.
42. In the 2012 BBC television production, *The Hollow Crown*, Ben Whishaw does manage to stab one of his murderers. But the use of longbows to shoot the imprisoned king from a distance and his transformation into an embarrassingly obvious type of St Sebastian, naked and pierced with arrows, seems like the culmination of a tradition that takes Richard too much at his own word, as he attempts to write his fate as a kind of martyrdom.
43. The implied stage directions contained in Richard's dialogue mean that he has to kill at least one person in this exchange of blows, as represented in the Oxford editors' interpolated stage direction. It may be, however, that he kills more than one, as other editors have decided. In the third Arden edition, for example, Charles Forker has him killing at least two, presumably taking

'another room' to indicate that he '*Kills another Servant*', dispatching two enemies to two different places in hell; William Shakespeare, *Richard II*, ed. Charles R. Forker (London: Cengage, 2002), 5.5.107s.d.

# Chapter 2

# Necks, Throats and Windpipes in *Henry V*: Sovereignty Translated

> One would then ask oneself: 'What is the theologico-political?' And the answer would take shape thus: the theologico-political is a system, an apparatus of sovereignty in which the death penalty is necessarily inscribed. There is theologico-political wherever there is death penalty.[1]

>         A damnèd death –
> Let gallows gape for dog, let man go free,
> And let no hemp his windpipe suffocate. (*Henry V*, 3.6.40–2)

I want to start my discussion of *Henry V* where I think all discussions of this play's politics should start: Norman Rabkin's 1977 essay, 'Rabbits, Ducks and *Henry V*'. Rabkin makes a compelling case for comparing *Henry V* to the *gestalt* picture of the 'rabbit-duck', arguing that the political attitude that characterises this play is generated by divergent, and seemingly incompatible, audience responses:

> Leaving the theatre at the end of the first performance, some members of the audience knew that they had seen a rabbit, others a duck. Still others, and I would suggest that they were Shakespeare's best audience, knew terrifyingly that they did not know what to think.[2]

The rabbit-duck analogy describes a play whose politics could be seen *either* as a rabbit that celebrates nationalist pride in heroic achievement, or as a duck that criticises Henry's Machiavellian manipulation of both friend and enemy. The two perspectives, as in the *gestalt* picture, cannot properly coincide other than in the schizoid response of 'Shakespeare's best audience' who turns out to be the literary critic, able to 'hold in balance incompatible and radically opposed views each of which seems exclusively true'.[3] But Rabkin's essay, brilliant as it is, does not entirely capture the ambivalences of *Henry V*, particularly when it comes to the play's representations of the workings of sovereignty. Rabkin is too much focused on the individual characteristics of the king, where much of the play's interest lies not so much in his personality but, rather, in the relationships and connections that he forges, or attempts to forge, with those whom he considers his subjects. This is, of course, a play about kingship, about what makes a good or a bad ruler, but it is much more a play about the workings of sovereignty, posing profound questions about where it is that the responsibility for decisions might lie. Whose fault is it when English soldiers die? Who decides who is the legitimate king? What, if any, rules and laws govern the actions of a monarch?

Maurice Hunt offers an alternative visual image to the 'rabbit-duck' that might give us a different template for interpreting the play. He offers the painting that has become a clichéd emblem for Renaissance duality, Holbein's *The Ambassadors*. This classic example of Renaissance perspective art famously offers its viewers the chance to step to the left-hand side of the painting and see the image of the two ambassadors, who are almost absurdly overloaded by the accoutrements of humanist and political achievement, recede into the background, as an anamorphic skull, otherwise seen as a blur of white and black paint, comes into focus. Hunt initially compares the way that we might read *Henry V* to this experience. Just as one version of Henry seems to move into view, then the other recedes into the background. However, Hunt rejects his own analogy and, by implication therefore, also Rabkin's *gestalt* picture; neither offers a genuine analogy for the jarring experience of considering King Henry to be both the perfect Christian prince and a cruel Machiavel at one and the same time. 'Viewing King Henry's character', Hunt writes, 'is not a matter of Renaissance perspective, for in this art one of the two possible contrary views is authoritative regardless of whether the viewer stands to one side or the other to view a perspective painting.'[4]

However, I don't think that Hunt is right about the Holbein painting. Sure, with the *gestalt* image you have to cancel out the rabbit in order to see the duck, and *vice versa*. It is hard, if not entirely impossible, to see both. But in the painting, the visual transaction that you make is of a very different order. One image, either the anamorphic skull or the ostentatious realism of the portrait, lingers on into and over the other, always leaving a residual blur behind. It is impossible to see the one visual plane without the other also being there; you always see them both, and the skull is never not visible, front and centre. As a visual experience, Holbein's painting resembles something more like an act of translation, rather than the ideal exchange of one thing for another, always imperfect and carrying with it traces of its process.

*Henry V* is a play that asks audiences and readers to think carefully about such transactions: one thing existing in place of, or alongside, or in exchange for, or as metonymic for, another: 'a kingdom for a stage' (Prologue.3), cannonballs for tennis balls, a 'nick' for a 'col', a French 'gorge' for an English 'throat', some 'brave crowns' instead of a cut throat, and being hanged by the neck as the judicial reward for stealing a 'pax of little price'. The *Henry IV* plays are more readily associated with the language of trade, commodity and exchange. Nina Levine has, for example, read those two plays as using economic language in a manner that shifts centres of power from crown to commons, from the court to the city: a centrifugal move coterminous with the development of corporations, as outlined by Henry Turner, and discussed in the Introduction. By reading the *Henry IV* plays for signs of everyday economic activity, she identifies 'a model of community that, in deriving its authority from everyday exchange rather than aristocratic ideals or from chronicle history is both more fluid and more heterogeneous that a "sceptered isle" of sacred rule'.[5]

That same language of everyday commercial activity is clearly not so present in *Henry V*, the world of the play being largely removed from the tavern setting that is so much a part of the *Henry IV* plays.[6] But there lingers, in this later play, a distinct concern with exchange through a focus on equivalences: what is equal to what? And the world of financial exigency is never far away. It is an important aspect of *Henry V*, right from the careful calculations of the two bishops, planning to buy off the king in a parliamentary debate that might see the Church losing much of its property, through to Pistol's plans at the end of the play to become a bawd, to 'steal' back to London, 'where I'll steal' (5.1.70). Such calculations are couched, though, in a broader and more abstract concern with exchange. In the famously self-reflexive aesthetic considerations of the opening Chorus, but also in its subject matter, the play asks questions about what is lost and what is gained in any given transaction, when any one thing is exchanged for, or changed into – translated into – any other.

In this chapter, I want to focus, then, not on the bifurcated reputation of Henry, as both hero and Machiavel, but on this idea of an incomplete translation, on the workings of sovereignty as never absolute but always leaving behind some remainder. The body part with which this becomes most associated in the play is perhaps unexpected: it is the neck, or the throat. This is a play concerned with translation or inadequate equivalences and, associated with this, also with the idea of capital punishment. When is judicial execution an adequate payment for offence, and how do forms of sovereignty underwrite the hanging of a thief?

Capital punishment, Derrida argues, is a determining factor for the existence of the 'theologico-political', for political theology:

One would then ask oneself: 'What is the theologico-political?' And the answer would take shape thus: the theologico-political is a system, an apparatus of sovereignty in which the death penalty in necessarily inscribed. There is theologico-political wherever there is death penalty.[7]

Identifying the death penalty as the 'hyphen in the theologico-political', Derrida explains capital punishment as an act that is always determined by a state that makes the claim that ultimate responsibility for justice originates beyond the state itself, usually divinely sanctioned. He begins his seminars on the death penalty with the contention that 'the death penalty, as the sovereign decision, is always the other's. Come from the other.'[8] Decisions over life and death, as decisions about exile, might be considered a defining characteristic of sovereign power, and yet these are also always decisions that it seems necessary to disavow, decisions from which individual kings distance themselves. Like Pontius Pilate, they wash their hands in a pretence that they, themselves, are only a cog in a mechanism that is beyond their control. The machinery of the death penalty, both metaphorical and sometimes literal, produces a system whereby agency is removed from the singular person of the king, or of any particular embodiment of the state: the blindfolded executioner; the machinery of the gallows; the claims to be meting out divine punishment rather than personal or political revenge.

In *Henry V*, the limits of sovereign agency are played out across the throats and necks of its characters. Whether by beheading or by hanging, it is the neck and throat of the criminal that is often the point of punishment. In both, it is also an attack on the head, the removal of the head from the body or the severing of ties between head and body. Capital punishment is punishment that relates to the *capita* – the head – and attacks the head of the criminal by means of the neck. I look at how the play treats capital punishment, establishing and working from the premise that *Henry V* is a play that conceives sovereign power with a particular relationship to capital punishment, before moving on to examine the play's extensive focus on the neck and throat.

## *Henry V* and Capital Punishment

It has not been recognised that *Henry V* is a play that is specifically – particularly even – interested in capital punishment. A play such as *Measure for Measure*, whose plot is measured out in anticipation of an execution, might offer itself up as a more concentrated meditation on judicial killing.[9] But executions mark key moments in the action of *Henry V* and in its ongoing investigation into the sovereign powers that attach themselves to Henry's kingship. First, there is the projected execution of the three conspirators, Scrope, Cambridge and Grey. Here, the traitors' insistence on the harsh treatment of a man for drunkenly 'railing' against the person of the king comes back to haunt them when their own treachery is discovered, and as Henry orders,

> Get ye therefore hence,
> Poor miserable wretches, to your death;
> The taste whereof, God of his mercy give
> You patience to endure, and true repentance
> Of all your dear offences. (2.3.172–6)

As elsewhere in the play, Henry seeks to make it understood that his sovereign decisions do not have their origins in his own person, nor depend on his personal wishes, but are, rather, the product of the workings of the state:

> Touching our person seek we no revenge,
> But we our kingdom's safety must so tender,
> Whose ruin you have sought, that to her laws
> We do deliver you. (2.3.169–72)

The perennial debate over Henry's apparent willingness, on the eve of Agincourt, to eschew blame for the fate of his soldiers should be read in relation to this earlier, comparable disavowal of responsibility for sovereign decisions that are, nonetheless, quite plainly associated with his 'person'. In the condemnation of the traitors, it is not at all clear that personal revenge is not the main motivation behind the king's actions. It is Scrope's betrayal of his position as Henry's bedfellow, his intimate companion, that most provokes his anger against the traitors. Any pretence of equanimity in the distinction that Henry makes between the harmless slanders of a drunkard and the real dangers of the conspirators' treachery is undermined by the vehemence of his criticism of Scrope. This is even demonstrated in Henry's use of pronouns in his speech to the traitors, where he modulates from the impersonal royal 'we' when he addresses Cambridge and Grey to a heartfelt 'I' when addressing Scrope. And elsewhere in the play, his eschewal of personal responsibility is compromised by the way that he inserts his own person into matters of state. So, for all of Henry's insistence that he cannot be held personally responsible for the souls of his soldiers, it is nevertheless through the emulation of his body that he attempts to mould them into soldiers, especially at the siege of Harfleur, and it is through inclusion into a highly personal 'brotherhood' that he hopes to inspire them to victory.

This imbrication of seemingly incompatible approaches, evident in the condemnation of the traitors – a paradox of personal intimacy and disavowal of responsibility – is also a feature of the other execution in the play, that of Bardolph, one of Henry's former drinking companions. For me, this is absolutely the emblematic moment of *Henry V*, as it concentrates into one episode many of the questions of sovereign agency and responsibility that feature throughout the play. And it does so with devastating pathos. Henry is told of the execution of his old friend by Fluellen who describes, in grotesquely comic terms, Bardolph's judicial maiming prior to execution, the slitting of his famously red nose:

> His face is all bubuncles and whelks and knobs and flames o'fire, and his lips blows at his nose, and it is like a coal of fire, sometimes plue and sometimes red. But his nose is executed, and his fire's out. (3.6.105–7)

The feature that most characterises Bardolph's intransigent failure fully to be incorporated into Henry's new model state, his resistance to being moved from the worlds of *Henry IV* into the less forgiving world of *Henry V*, is his extravagantly alcoholic complexion. But this is, in Fluellen's unsympathetic blazon, now put to service in a demonstration of Henry's sovereign power. And Henry describes the execution as a fair exchange, an exercise in just equivalence, as exemplary justice from which he almost manages to remove his own agency (even as that agency is asserted): 'We would have all offenders so cut off' (3.6.108). This use of the impersonal, royal 'we' is habitual for Henry in ways that it is not for any other of Shakespeare's kings. He very rarely breaks out of it to use the first person at any length, with key exceptions being, as I mentioned, to Scrope as he condemns his personal treachery, in his violent threats to the besieged governor of Harfleur, at the start of the St Crispin's Day speech when his 'we' expands to include those 'happy few' that he addresses, and throughout his talk with Catherine as he seals their marriage in the final scene. However, in his condemnation of the convicted Bardolph, given what we know of the personal history between the two men, his characteristic use of 'we' seems even more particularly marked. And the generalisation of 'all such offenders' paired with the passive construction 'so cut off' further distances him from any personal stake in the hanging of this petty thief.

However, what lingers across our view in contemplating this, for Henry, justified and even-handed punishment is the more visceral and significantly less comic description of Bardolph's execution offered by Pistol a few lines earlier:

> Fortune is Bardolph's foe and frowns on him,
> For he hath stol'n a pax, and hangèd must a be.
> A damnèd death –
> Let gallows gape for dog, let man go free,
> And let no hemp his windpipe suffocate.
> But Exeter hath given the doom of death
> For pax of little price.
> Therefore go speak, the Duke will hear thy voice,
> And let not Bardolph's vital thread be cut
> With edge of penny cord and vile reproach. (3.6.31–41)

Pistol is attempting to persuade Fluellen to intercede for his friend but, in marked contrast to the brotherly nation that Henry sometimes seeks to promote, Fluellen confirms that 'if, look you, he were my brother, I would desire the Duke to use his good pleasure, and put him to execution' (3.6.44–6). Fluellen's refusal to intervene is a similar disavowal (while enacting) sovereign power to Henry's 'we would have all such offenders so cut off'.

But Pistol refutes the judicial book-keeping that has been underwritten by Henry (a hanging as equivalent to 'a pax of little price'), and points rather towards their lack of justification. He offers a substitution of a different sort ('Let gallows gape for dog, let man go free') and presents us with the remainder (the remains) in this equation of sovereign justice: the windpipe crushed by the rough hemp of the rope that is as cheap as the little crucifix that Bardolph is accused of stealing. As Gillian Kendall writes of representations of execution in Shakespearean drama, 'The body offers resistance to inflicted suffering; it wishes to live.'[10] Pistol's account of the execution is both poignant in the claims that it makes for the emptiness of the gesture of executing this small-time pilferer, and bitterly sardonic in its evident attack on what he sees as the iniquitous workings of justice. At the heart of his speech is an idea of inappropriate exchange, or of failed equivalences. And the language he turns to is economic, perhaps reminding us of the financial transactions between Church and crown that had initially established the grounds for war at the start of the play. As Jeffrey Knapp has argued, 'the marked contrast between Bardolph's petty theft and the enormous sum that Henry extorted from the church does make Bardolph's punishment seem excessively harsh'.[11]

Bardolph's lack of 'fortune', of course, alludes to luck rather than money, but, as the speech continues, it is clear that the two are linked and there is a strong implication that Bardolph's execution is as much the product of poverty as it is of bad luck. When Pistol claims that the pax that Bardolph stole was 'of little price', he makes a very specific point that alludes more to contemporary Elizabethan London than to military justice in the field during the Hundred Years' War. From the fourteenth century onwards, the theft of property worth less than a shilling was not a capital offence. J. A. Sharpe writes that, as inflation caught up with this amount during the sixteenth century, courts started to undervalue the cost of stolen goods to ensure that accused thieves were not executed if they had only stolen goods 'of little price'.[12] Notwithstanding this apparent get-out clause, the reigns of Elizabeth I and James I were a high point in the use of hanging as a punishment in England. Sharpe shows that the customary attention to the eighteenth century, with the arrival of the harsh 'Bloody Code' under which hanging was made much more widely available as a punishment for property offences, obscures the fact that 'the first wave of legislative harshness and the rise in the number of capital convictions, occurred around the middle of the sixteenth century', subsiding in the mid-seventeenth century.[13]

If Derrida is right that capital punishment is the hyphen connecting the theologico-political, then to reimagine execution as, in part, a form of exchange is to begin to pull those two terms apart. Bardolph's execution, in Pistol's description, exceeds the demands made on the life of his erstwhile friend by Henry's royal we on behalf of 'our kingdom'. Rather, the event is rendered significant in an economy that is described in financial terms that undermine the centralising claims of Henry's disingenuous disavowal of responsibility, a disavowal that is designed to protect the privilege of sovereign decisionism from critique. As discussed earlier, it is in *Homo Sacer* that Agamben attempts to provide the corollary to the extra-legal status of the sovereign exception, as found in political theology, in the idea of a life that is vulnerable to death but not contained within the judicial system. What we see with Bardolph is something quite different to this: yes, his is a life contained within the judicial system, but this is a system that is imagined – at least by Pistol – as not necessarily coterminous with the world. Or rather, Shakespeare's exploration of the moment of his death in Pistol's speech affords it a meaning that exceeds Henry's claims to the body via his sovereign decision and the death sentence that this decision underwrites.

In a later book – *The Kingdom and the Glory* – Agamben takes his argument to the metaphysical conception of sovereignty itself, unpicking it through its reliance on (or production through) forms of deputation. This occasionally seems as if it might be something more like Derrida's deconstruction of the self-sameness of sovereignty, 'said and supposed to be indivisible but always divisible'.[14] In this last of Agamben's trilogy of books on sovereignty, he traces what appears to be something more like 'governmentality' back to the economy of the Christian trinity, as itself always divided, always produced through forms of deputisation and through the separation of powers between capacity and use, between executive and instrumental branches:

> The theological model of the separation of power from its exercise is found in the distinction between the absolute and ordered power [*potenza*] in God – that is, in the doctrine of divine impotence, of what God, in spite of his omnipotence, cannot do (or cannot not do).[15]

But for all Agamben's attempt in this book to account for the dissemination of power, the double negative that concludes this sentence further traps sovereignty within the Bodinian and Schmittian concept of the exception. And his 'cannot not do' is also uncannily reminiscent of Henry's multiple eschewals of agency in *Henry V*, including his 'We would have all offenders so cut off'. Henry makes claims to a form of 'divine impotence' (he cannot not do other than what he is doing) even as his claims to a form of absolutist sovereignty appear to be realised through the execution of his former friend. And this is the second friend that he cannot help but execute – he cannot not execute – in the play.

And yet Pistol's commentary opens up the play's ideas of exchange and economy in quite different directions, and within an economy that is not so trapped as that imagined by Agamben in *The Kingdom and the Glory*. If concepts of sovereignty grounded within political theology are dependent on the obfuscation of agency that emerges within the exception, and if capital punishment is the defining event within this system ('to her laws / We do deliver you'), then Pistol's powerful and pathos-laden commentary lays bare the violent mechanisms of such non-agential sovereign agency. Or rather, Shakespeare's continually restless metaphorisations of the body still dislocate sovereignty from any secure basis in the excepted person of the monarch, even in this seemingly king-obsessed play.

## Translating the Neck in *Henry V*

The processes of exchange that are foregrounded most often in *Henry V* are acts of translation. The scene in which the French princess, Catherine, starts on her course towards becoming an English queen by learning the English words for French body parts is the most obvious example of a constant issue the play has with cross-cultural interpretation and misinterpretation.

CATHERINE Comment appelez-vous le col?
ALICE *De nick*, madame. (3.4.28–30)

As with her other translations in this scene, Alice's mispronunciation of the English word 'neck' as 'nick' introduces a bawdy sense, sometimes understood and acknowledged by the French women and sometimes not. Here 'nick' for 'neck' is, like other words for cuts, apertures and indentations (the 'cranny' in *A Midsummer Night's Dream*; in *The Winter's Tale* the 'crack' that Leontes sees in Hermione; Gloucester's 'fault' in the opening scene of *King Lear*; or the left shoe with the hole in it from *Two Gentleman of Verona*), a reference to female genitals. The schoolboy humour of this pun is part of the more general economy of translation in which definitions are inevitably inexact, always both lacking and in excess. Other examples of this kind of thing in the play would have to include the Welsh mispronunciations of English words by Fluellen, whose name, at least in the printed speech prefixes, is an Anglicised misspelling of the Welsh Llewelyn.

In Catherine's English lesson, the 'nick' is just one body part among several, but the neck, or rather the 'throat', is, as well as being an important part of the play's focus on capital punishment, something that is translated into and out of French elsewhere in the play. In the early scenes, Nim threatens to cut Pistol's throat for marrying Nell Quickly when she had been betrothed to him. Sardonically, he tells Bardolph that he might come at Pistol when he is asleep:

> Things must be as they may. Men may sleep, and they may have their throats about them at that time, and some say knives have edges. It must be as it may. (2.1.19–22)

Then, when he has Pistol in his sights, he openly threatens to 'cut thy throat'. Pistol responds, '*Couple a gorge*, / That is the word' (2.1.66–9). Pistol's mispronounced, or misspelled, French is odd. It is not odd that it is mispronounced or misspelled. That is, as Gary Taylor argues, likely to be the folio compositor's error rather than an extension of the mispronunciations of words foreign to the speaker that are so much a feature of the rest of the play (2.1.68n). Rather, it is odd that in exchanging 'coupe' or 'couper' for 'couple', he confutes two opposites: cutting and joining (coupling). Katherine's exchange of 'neck' for 'nick' may be a piece of bawdy, but it also plays with the idea of the neck's vulnerability to being cut elsewhere in the play.

Pistol's '*couple a gorge*' also pre-empts the 'once more unto the breach' speech, with its announcement of violent conjunctions of splitting/breaching with closing ('close the wall up with our English dead').

The severing of throats in this play, whether in the service of judicial punishment or within the violent regimes of war, considers the throat, or the neck, as a site of exchange, transfer and translation. In exchanging his English 'throat' for a French '*gorge*', Pistol may already be preparing himself for the journey to war. And, certainly, this is a phrase that comes in handy for him in a later scene of translation between English and French. On the battlefield, Pistol has a boy translate his intentions towards a defeated French soldier:

> PISTOL Bid him prepare, for I will cut his throat.
> FRENCH SOLDIER *Que dit-il, monsieur?*
> BOY *Il me commande à vous dire que vous faites vous prêt, car ce soldat ici est disposé tout à cette heure de couper votre gorge.*
> PISTOL *Oui, couper la gorge, par ma foi,*
> Peasant, unless thou give me crowns, brave crowns;
> Or mangled shalt thou be by this my sword. (4.4.29–35)

In *Henry V*, acts of translation are performed over and through the body, whether the eroticised body of the French princess or, here, the body of a prisoner of war: French gorges for English throats; French throats in return for (anachronistic) English crowns.

Pistol's threat to 'mangle' his captive's throat with his sword is a telling choice of word for this play. This word is picked up in the devastatingly ironic final chorus, the sonnet that forms the epilogue:

> Thus far with rough and all-unable pen
>   Our bending author hath pursued the story,
> In little room confining mighty men,
>   Mangling by starts the full course of their glory. (Epilogue.1–4)

It is not entirely clear what the subject of the verb 'mangle' is in this chorus. Has the playwright 'mangled' the story, or have the heroes of the story been seen to 'mangle' their own 'glory' through acts that might be understood as less than glorious? The play and the 'mighty men' both progress 'by starts', erratically and out of sync. 'Mangle' becomes a word through which the various transactions or transformations that occur in this play are imagined and projected. The Duke of Burgundy refers to the peace brokered between France and England at the close of the play as a 'mangled peace' (5.2.34). If the scene is described by Burgundy as a kind of mirror image, or even a kind of mathematical equation – 'face to face and royal eye to eye' (5.2.30) – the words 'mangling' and 'mangle' denote a lack of equivalence in exchange and representation. With the word 'mangle', equivalence is reimagined as a kind of lack. It does this through and over the bodies of actors and characters, highlighting the 'gap' between actor and part, as well as the ironic discrepancies in the transaction itself. 'Mangle' is *Henry V*'s equivalent word for *Henry VI* part one's 'gimmers': the realisation of a disarticulated 'body politic'.

One final bit of throat cutting: Henry's order that French prisoners have their throats cut in revenge for the French killing of English boys, left behind in camp, is described by Gower:

> 'Tis certain there's not a boy left alive. And the cowardly rascals that ran from the battle ha' done this slaughter. Besides, they have burned and carried away all that was in the King's tent; wherefore the King most worthily hath caused every soldier to cut his prisoner's throat. O 'tis a gallant king. (4.7.5–10)

Gower justifies Henry's actions as a matter of evident equivalence: because ('wherefore') the French have burned his luggage (in another example of ill-fitting equivalence, this does seem to be the most immediate cause rather than the killing of the boys), he has 'most worthily' had their compatriots' throats cut. In underlining Gower's sense that Henry's order is a righteous one, Fluellen responds with yet another 'mangled' comparison, asking Gower the name of the town where 'Alexander the Pig was born' (4.7.12–13), preparing to offer his king as a belated avatar of the Macedonian hero. Gower corrects him with 'Alexander the Great' but Fluellen refuses to see the difference:

> Why I pray you, is not 'pig' great? The pig or the great or the huge or the magnanimous are all one reckonings, save the phrase is a little variations. (4.7.15–17)

Having, to his mind, proven the effective exchange value of 'pig' with 'great', save only a 'little variations', he then proceeds to argue for the absolute equivalence between Macedon, the birthplace of Alexander the Pig, and Monmouth, the town in Wales where Henry was born. Fluellen's rather slapdash attitude towards equivalences, translations, calculations and 'reckonings' is only seemingly out of kilter with a play that is otherwise very concerned with counting and multiplying, from the 'cipher' in the opening chorus to the accounts of the French outnumbering the English on the eve of Agincourt and the balance sheet of the dead at the end of battle. Fluellen's indifference to these differences is a particularly stark realisation of the imbalance and the lack of equivalence in all these kinds of transactions and equivalences throughout the play. As with the word 'mangling', the ironic versions of equivalence offered in Fluellen's analogies draw attention to an error (a 'start') in the transactions of the play. It is the trace of the skull in Holbein's *Ambassadors*, even as you refocus on the main body of the picture.

In tracing these ironies of equivalence and in representation and exchange, I am adding to a long critical history of this play that pays attention to the way that its aesthetic questions, around the adequacy or inadequacy of theatrical representation, can be linked to its ambiguous politics. But why does the play focus so much on the neck and throat? The persistent attention paid to this particular body part is generated by the play's interest in capital punishment. The king's sentence on the condemned traitors appears to instantiate a decisionist form of sovereignty, but the dialogue of *Henry V* continually couches such claims within languages of exchange, translation and uneven equivalences. The remainder of these exchanges is always the human body, in pieces, what Eric Santner refers to as 'the surplus secreted' when, to invoke Aristotle and Agamben after Santner, *zoe* is transformed into *bios*, biological flesh into political personhood, and matter into representation. Here – what do we find – 'bare life' or prosthstatics; flesh or representation; 'natural' man or 'artificial'?

One of the dominant questions of the history plays is that of participation: to what extent does any one body participate in, form part of, or fall outside of, the body politic? In this play, the translations and transactions that take hold of the 'throat' are a means through which that question can be asked. Nim prepares for France and he and his compatriots retrain their cut-throat knives on Frenchmen rather than on each other; and Catherine, the French princess, learns to redescribe her body as that of Henry's wife. The throats of Frenchmen are mangled in return for the lives of young English boys. These events, and their figuration through the translated throat, work out patterns of belonging and incorporation within the nation-state. This translation of Shakespeare's dismembered body parts into national history poses questions about the legitimacy of war and of sovereign justice. On the eve of Agincourt, Henry V is presented by the sceptical Williams with a vision of these mangled bodies reassembled to call Henry to account:

> But if the cause be not good, the King himself hath a heavy *reckoning* to make, when all these legs and arms and heads chopped off in a battle shall join together at the latter day, and cry all, 'We died at such a place.' (4.1.129–32; my emphasis)

This is a vision of the apocalypse, but also an equation of sorts: another 'reckoning'. This is a very different vision of transformed body parts to that invited by Henry himself at the siege of Harfleur, where he co-opts the sinews, eyes, brows, teeth, nostrils, breath and blood of his soldiers for a project of reinvigorating the national body politic. But in both, body parts are listed in such a way that questions are asked about the conditions within which individuals might be said to participate in the state, and the extent to which the crown itself might become the ultimate arbiter of equivalence and incorporation. In the next chapter, as I move from the neck, vulnerable to axe, knife and 'penny rope', to the hand, these questions are asked still more urgently, this time in relation to individual agency. Is your hand ever really your own? This is a question posed relentlessly in the dialogue and action of *King John*, a play in which hands come to seem less like a metonym of personal will, and something more like a prosthetic attachment.

## Notes

1. Jacques Derrida, *The Death Penalty*, volume I, ed. Geoffrey Bennington, Marc Crépon and Thomas Dutoit, trans. Peggy Kamuf (Chicago: University of Chicago Press, 2014), p. 23.
2. Norman Rabkin, 'Rabbits, Ducks, and *Henry V*', *Shakespeare Quarterly* 28.3 (1977), p. 285.
3. Rabkin, 'Rabbits, Ducks, and *Henry V*', p. 285.
4. Maurice Hunt, 'The "Breaches" of Shakespeare's *The Life of King Henry the Fifth*', *College Literature* 41.4 (2014), pp. 7–24.
5. Nina Levine, 'Extending Credit in the *Henry IV* Plays', *Shakespeare Quarterly* 51.4 (2000), p. 404. Levine identifies a tendency, even as critics identify the presence of 'sixteenth-century commerce' in the play, to relate it to the politics of the crown. I am, undoubtedly, repeating that tendency. Benjamin Bertram has also identified, in the *Henry IV* plays, discursive congruities and incongruities between a language of exchange and the language of state politics. I will pick this up in my later chapter on those plays. Benjamin Bertram, 'Falstaff's Body, the Body Politic, and the Body of Trade', *Exemplaria* 21.3 (2009), pp. 296–318.
6. In my chapter on the *Henry IV* plays, I foreground Shakespeare's seemingly out-of-control addiction to rhetorical *copia*, another aspect of these plays' movement away from unitary centres of power.
7. Derrida, *The Death Penalty*, p. 23.
8. Derrida, *The Death Penalty*, p. 1.
9. See Gillian Murray Kendall, 'Overkill in Shakespeare', *Shakespeare Quarterly* 43.1 (1992), pp. 33–50; and Huw Griffiths, 'Hotel Rooms and Bodily Fluids in Two Recent Productions of *Measure for Measure*, Or, Why Barnardine is Still Important', *Shakespeare Bulletin* 32.4 (2014), pp. 559–83.
10. Kendall, 'Overkill in Shakespeare', p. 34.
11. Jeffrey Knapp, 'Preachers and Players in Shakespeare's England', *Representations* 44 (autumn 1993), p. 39.
12. Sharpe writes that 'by the seventeenth century large numbers of thieves were escaping the gallows due to the deliberate undervaluing by the courts of the goods they had stolen', in order to mitigate the effects of inflation;

J. A. Sharpe, *Judicial Punishment in England* (London: Faber and Faber, 1990), p. 24.
13. Sharpe, *Judicial Punishment*, p. 31.
14. Derrida, *The Beast and the Sovereign*, vol. I, p. 291.
15. Agamben, *The Kingdom and the Glory*, p. 104.

Chapter 3

# Prosthetic Hands in *King John*

Any relation is a relation to difference or otherness, and prosthesis is a name for that.[1]

This chapter proceeds by first establishing a relationship between the figure of synecdoche and early modern conceptions of sovereignty. This connection helps to explain why it is that Shakespeare's interest in compromised and attenuated claims to sovereign power gathers, in *King John*, around the body part of the 'hand'. The word 'hand' is obsessively repeated in the dialogue of the play, usually as a synecdoche that implies something about personal agency. With a remarkable forty-six uses of 'hand', *King John* contains more instances of the word than any other of Shakespeare's plays, including the obvious runner-up, *Titus Andronicus*, which has thirty-nine.[2] The status of the hand as either synecdoche or, as it comes to seem, almost as a form of prosthetic attachment reveals *King John* as one of Shakespeare's most searching investigations of the suppositions of the supposedly inalienable nature of sovereign power. Farah Karim Cooper writes of the idea of the hand that it is 'the instrument with which we engage with the physical world and it is the part of our body, apart from the face, with which we communicate most expressively and passionately'.[3] To the extent that this is correct, it assumes that your hand is your own, but sometimes it isn't. Sometimes, you might be obliged to act as a deputy for somebody else, to place their will above yours. And, in *King John* as with other plays, a Bodinesque insistence on integrated, inalienable and absolute forms of sovereignty is something that, while entertained at times, is ultimately unsustainable. What is more, this play's investigation of personal responsibility provides a platform for asking some of the fundamental questions of political thought, such as 'when is it acceptable to kill somebody on command?' In this, Shakespeare's work prefigures that of Hobbes. Hobbes's *Leviathan* presents a version of sovereign power in which a prior decision is always assumed to have been made whereby subjects have yielded their individual will to that of the sovereign or, rather, to the state *as* sovereign, most readily imagined by Hobbes as a single figure: the king.

And yet, in the mechanics of power that Hobbes extrapolates from this primary political scene, contradictions emerge that afford the assimilated subject some form of exceptional power that might stand outside the absolute claims of the sovereign. These exceptions are most clearly present in a refusal to kill on behalf of the sovereign, a refusal that is reserved for subjects deputised to do so in some circumstances. In *King John*, Shakespeare plays this scenario out around fifty years before Hobbes theorises it during the civil wars. In particular, the relationship between King John and Hubert, wherein the king deputises his subject to kill Prince Arthur on his behalf, becomes an illustration of the alienability of sovereign power, rather than its inherence within the body of the monarch. Even as King John asserts his will over his subject, Hubert, that will is complicatedly mediated through a chain of synecdochal 'hands' that operate in a manner that Derrida would term 'prosthstatic'. The linguistic corollary for prosthesis is synecdoche.

### 'Borrowed majesty': Synecdochal Sovereignty

Hillman and Mazzio have written that 'Insofar as parts were imagined as dominant vehicles for the articulation of culture, the early modern period could be conceptualized as an age of synecdoche.'[4] Synecdoche has a significant contribution to make to the way in which we think about sovereignty. When, in *The Arte of English Poesie*, George Puttenham defines this elusive figure ('the figure of quick conceit') he uses two examples that are about contests over sovereignty. The first relates to Spanish rule in the Low Countries: 'if one would say, the town of Andwerpe were famished, it is not so to be taken, but of the people of the town of Andwerp'.[5] Puttenham's 'Andwerpe' (Antwerp) echoes an example given by Cicero in *de Oratore*, this time for the related figure of metonymy. Cicero quotes the *Annals*, Ennius' fragmentary epic of Roman history: 'Africa's quivering now that it trembles with terrible turmoil'.[6] Like 'Andwerpe', the proper name 'Africa' stands for its inhabitants in a synecdochal relationship, one being an aspect of, or part of, the other. But also like the Antverpians, Cicero's Africans are caught up in violent activities that produce physical suffering (fear and starvation) because of the way that their bodies have come to participate in a violent conflict, because of the extent to which they *are* 'Africa' or

'Andwerpe'. For the Antverpians, this is the Spanish siege of 1585 that starved them into submission; for Cicero and Ennius, the Africans are 'trembling' in response to Scipio's campaigns.

These examples reveal something of the difficulty of maintaining any secure distinction between synecdoche and metonymy. Puttenham believes that synecdoche can either involve a part being taken for a whole, or be where the whole is taken for a part. Other definitions might suggest that synecdoche refers only to parts in the place of wholes, whereas metonymy might name a wider set of figures in which aspects, parts, sets and subsets are enabled to stand in one for the other. It is Puttenham's definition of synecdoche in which I am most interested. This is not because I believe him to be authoritative in the classification of rhetorical tropes, but because this flexible interpretation of synecdoche – alternating between parts and wholes – is useful when questions emerge around the distribution of sovereign power: crowns standing in for kings; specific populations standing in for larger ideas of the nation and so on. In the examples given here, both Puttenham's synecdoche and Cicero's metonymy work through the incorporation of bodies into larger narratives of sovereign control.

In a further example of what Puttenham identifies as synecdoche, the structures of sovereign participation are at work from the opposite end of the hierarchy. But this participation is still thought through in terms of bodies standing in for – deputising for – other bodies, parts of the polity that are both incorporated and, at the same time, detached and isolated: 'as when one would tell me how the French king was overthrown at Saint Quintans, I am enforced to think that it was not the king himselfe in person, but the Constable of Fraunce with the French kings power'.[7] Here, the 'Constable of Fraunce' both is, and is not, the same thing as the 'French king'. The deputy both is, and is not, sovereign. Puttenham is obviously concerned in some way with whether or not the deputy, the 'Constable', can, in some circumstances, be called 'king' or, at least, 'France', as itself an aspect not so much of the nation as of the sovereignty inherent in the title, 'King of France'. In these synecdochal forms, sovereign power is made manifest in the form of a transaction, the 'person' of the French king serving only as a notional depository of sovereign power that is, in effect, always on the move. The singular 'person' of the king is never enough to figure a sovereign power that is always located elsewhere. It is interesting, and not, I think, coincidental, that Puttenham's example of a political synecdoche is situated in France; it was from the French wars of religion and their subsequent theorisation that the most urgent and significant political questions emerged, particularly through resistance theory and in the absolutism of Bodin.

There are two ways in which an inherent potential for political restlessness might be controlled in early modern conceptions of sovereignty. One would be through heredity: a kingship that transcends individuals through the continuity of blood and dynasty. This can be underwritten either by reference to 'divine right' or a metaphysics of royal blood: power handed over to a particular individual either from God to man, or from sovereign to sovereign. The other is through formalising and centralising processes of deputisation, such that executive political power might be understood only in relation to its origins in a single sovereign body. This latter is what motivates the mainstream of absolutist thought in the period, from Bodin to Hobbes, and is also something that motivates the plot of Shakespeare's *King John*, although, as I will show later in this chapter, the play has some interesting things to say about heredity as well.

Synecdoche and the related figure of metonymy have, then, a particular role to play in conceptions of sovereign authority and power. This relationship is established through a shared discourse of participation and detachment: what does it mean to be a part, or an aspect, of something? Or, what does it mean to be deputised? One of the central questions in any consideration of sovereignty is the extent to which any one person's body, whether king, subject or citizen, can be said to be a part of – to participate in, to be parasitically incorporated into, or prosthetically attached to – a larger 'body politic'. To whom, or what, does your body belong? You, as an individual, or the state? Whereas it might be thought that synecdoche could work to stabilise the inbuilt unpredictability of sovereign power through a language of belonging, tying people and bodies securely into ideas that exist beyond them (kingship, divine right, nationhood, blood), this is not how it works out in practice. Shakespeare's synecdochal body parts, including *King John*'s 'hands', tend to denote a failure fully to provide a secure, integrated, sovereign body. The syntagmatic (one thing leading on to another) rather than paradigmatic (one thing relating to another through analogy) nature of synecdoche is always more likely to convey conceptions of sovereignty that do not readily locate it in one single body but, rather, disperse it through various agencies.

Roman Jakobson's influential definition of metonymy as dependent on 'contiguity' as opposed to the 'similarity' that is posited by metaphor is helpful, but not quite adequate. While I take from this the related terms 'syntagmatic' and 'paradigmatic' to discuss the difference between metonymy and metaphor, and while Jakobson's 'metonymy' might describe the proximal relationships being imagined here (Antverpians are *near* Antwerp rather than *like* Antwerp), his theory fails to imagine the senses of incorporation, connection and disconnection that are a key feature of the synecdochal relations of sovereignty in which parts and wholes are never attached neutrally but, rather, related in power-charged contexts of assimilation and disavowal. The term 'syntagmatic' offers a compelling way of thinking about the proximal relations involved in Shakespeare's particularly transactional versions of sovereignty, but it does not quite do justice to the potential violence involved in being incorporated or alienated. Kings and their agents are never just *next* to each other. Puttenham's anxious attempt to demarcate where the power of the King of France resides – in his own (absent) person or in the defeated 'Constable of Fraunce' – bespeaks a concern in early modern considerations of sovereign power as to whether sovereignty *could* be deputised or transferred in some way, or whether it was inalienable and indivisible. This concern is dynamically taken up by Shakespeare in his Elizabethan history plays. The persistent response of these plays is that sovereignty is always in the process of being dispersed and transferred. The idea of a sovereignty that is absolutely inalienable is not supported by the dramatic action, or by the various representations of sovereign power and authority seen in any of these plays.

In *King John*, this is demonstrated with particular intensity. Here, the synecdoche that most often foregrounds questions about sovereign capacity is the 'hand', the hand both as a body part and as an aspect or representation of individual agency. However, this is a hand that, at times, seems so susceptible to alienation from the intentions of its owner that it might also be usefully thought of as a kind of prosthetic attachment, as well as a complex synecdoche for a person's intentions and willed action. Through this focus on the 'hand', *King John* articulates a vision of sovereign authority and sovereign power that is always on the move, always being handed over and located elsewhere. It never inheres in the mystical body of the monarch him- or herself.

The opening dialogue of *King John* immediately focuses attention on the locations of sovereign power, and the question that the audience is repeatedly asked to consider is the nature of 'majesty', and whether it can be 'borrowed'.[8] 'Majesty', a significant word in *King John*, is also a key term in early modern conceptions of sovereignty. Its associations, emerging most strongly in the absolutist theories of Bodin, are usually with the discrete, and supposedly inviolable, person of the sovereign. But in the confrontation that opens *King John*, the king is accused by Châtillon, the French ambassador, of having '*borrowed* majesty'. This phrase is made particularly resonant by the way that it is then elaborated on in the remainder of the play's opening dialogue. First, Châtillon introduces it as a pointed qualification, self-consciously advertising his use of *correctio* as a way to insult King John:

> Thus, after greeting, speaks the King of France,
> In my behaviour, to the majesty,
> The borrowed majesty, of England here. (1.1.2–4)

Châtillon's overt use of *correctio* (not 'majesty' but '*borrowed* majesty') leads to further emphasis being given to the phrase when Queen Eleanor, the king's mother, picks up on it and repeats it back to the messenger as a question:

> A strange beginning – 'borrowed majesty'? (1.1.5)

This repetition ensures that, as King John silences his mother ('Silence, good mother, hear the embassy', 1.1.6), this 'strange beginning' of a 'borrowed majesty' lingers on as a question mark, determining the tenor of the ensuing debate and of the entire play. The questions being asked are not simply those about the legitimacy of John's own specific claim to the English throne – something that is always in doubt; more speculative questions about sovereignty and embodiment are also being proposed: to whom, and where, does 'majesty' belong? Can it be transferred? Can it be divided? If it can be 'borrowed', can it be returned? Or, given the sarcasm with which Châtillon and Queen Eleanor both load the phrase, the implication might be that 'borrowed majesty' is an impossible paradox, an oxymoron even. The word itself, 'borrowed', draws on a financial vocabulary of mutual exchange that runs counter to the implications of 'majesty'. Perhaps they have read their Bodin, and they are implying that 'majesty', if it is to retain its true significance, simply cannot be 'borrowed'; moreover, they are suggesting, it is not something that can be moved in any way: it cannot be translated, divided or transferred.

'Majesty' – the refrain from *King John*'s opening lines – is one of Bodin's main hooks for securing his understanding of sovereignty. In glossing his well-known definition of sovereignty as 'the absolute and perpetual power of a commonwealth', he uses the Latin term 'maiestas'.[9] Later in the *Six Books of the Commonwealth*, he returns to the concept of majesty and insists that it can only apply to a power whose sovereignty is inalienable:

> As for the title 'majesty,' it is clear enough that it belongs only to someone who is sovereign. Some rulers also take the title 'sacred majesty' like the [German] emperor, others 'excellent majesty,' like the queen of England in her edicts and letters patent . . .[10]

'Majesty', in Bodin, might be characterised as exceptional ('sacred', 'excellent') but could certainly never admit of being 'borrowed' and transferred, or of being in any way doubled or replicable.

In these opening exchanges of the play, Châtillon, as he does elsewhere, speaks on behalf of the French king who is, in turn, acting as an agent for young Prince Arthur, the actual claimant to the English throne. It might be thought, on this account, that if anyone in this scene is 'borrowing' his 'majesty', then it is either Châtillon or his master, King Philip. When Châtillon talks about handing sovereignty over to Arthur, he does refer to it as a portable object, a sword that can be moved from 'hand' to 'hand'. He tells the English court that Philip of France, speaking 'in right and true behalf' of Arthur (so Châtillon speaking for Philip speaking for Arthur), lays claim to the crown:

> Desiring thee to lay aside the sword
> Which sways usurpingly over these several titles,
> And put the same into young Arthur's hand,
> Thy nephew, and right royal sovereign. (1.1.12–15)

In *King John*, the synecdoche of the 'hand' (this is its first use in the play) is the locus of an investigation into sovereign authority, and its relationship to political agency. The 'hand' – both the word and the body part itself – is the focal point around which circulate the play's pressing questions about where sovereign authority is located, how that authority might be transferred, and the legitimacy of political action.

There are several aspects of *King John* that pose questions of sovereignty, particularly of sovereign agency. These include the conflict over the crown itself, a conflict which encompasses King John's peculiar second coronation, and also the figure of the Bastard, that representation of oddly attenuated sovereignty. The questions around agency, sovereignty and deputisation come to a head, however, in the instructions that Hubert is given to kill Prince Arthur, and in the ensuing complications around the 'accidental' death of the young prince. This sequence of events focuses attention throughout the middle of the play on what it means to act on behalf of, or in place of, a monarch, and it is also this episode which features the biggest concentration of the synecdochal/prosthetic 'hand' that is so much a feature of the whole play.

The 'hand' is taken up by plays other than *King John*, as a way of thinking about the location of sovereignty. In *Richard II*, when Richard abdicates, he imagines that, while he can give up the trappings of sovereignty (sceptre, crown, balm, 'duteous oaths'), he might retain some sense of himself as being in possession of sovereign authority. The famous abdication scene achieves much of its pathos from the tension between

Richard's domination of the theatrical performance and the character's lack of control over the transactions of sovereignty. Sovereignty, here, no more rests in the person of Richard than it does in the crown. It lies, rather, in the capacity to control Richard's hand as it transfers crown and sceptre from one person to another. This is a hand that, at this point, hardly belongs to Richard at all and is certainly no longer an extension of his sovereign will. Sovereign authority might, in some sense, be seen as located still in the person of Richard, but this is utterly divorced from sovereign power, from his capacity to act. When he says, 'With mine own hands I give away my crown', the excessive focus on the possessive ('mine', 'own', 'my') pointedly underlines the dispossession that is, in fact, taking place. His hands, here, are no more his own than is the crown. Ultimately, in this scene, sovereignty is not located in the mystical body of Richard or, indeed, in its coupling, via the figure of the 'king's two bodies', with a transcendent 'majesty'. Rather, it is in motion; it is all in the transaction. A focus on synecdochal body parts, such as hands in *King John* and *Richard II*, is one way of realising this in the theatre, locating the movement of bodies and props on stage in a language that presents the body of the sovereign as never quite intact.

For Bodin, deputisation could never really involve 'borrowing' majesty but is, rather, to be understood as a temporary and highly curtailed 'granting' of power that in no way divides or dissipates the originary 'person of the sovereign'. In fact, it legitimates the sovereign still more; sovereignty sustains itself by granting powers to other people which it, nevertheless, retains. Whatever power the sovereign appears to give away, she or he keeps back still more power in reserve. Puttenham's synecdoche that has the 'Constable of Fraunce' as participating in the identity of the King of France would not really be compatible with this Bodinesque form of deputising. If it were aligned with the way that I was writing about synecdoche, Bodin's understanding of sovereignty might be said to be resolutely *paradigmatic* rather than *syntagmatic*. Where, for Bodin, a deputy's authority might *resemble* the authority of the sovereign (as in, for example, a metaphor), it does not partake in that authority in a way that might, instead, constitute either sharing sovereign agency or dispersing it. Deputies, in this model, are metaphors for, rather than synecdochal with, kings; one is a paradigm or analogy for the other rather than being syntagmatic with it. What *King John* reveals, however, is the instability and unsustainability of Bodin's model, illustrating the always dependent status of sovereign agency, and its emergence in transfers of power rather than in an 'excepted' or extra-legal condition.

As we have seen already, Bodin, in refuting resistance theories associated with the Huguenots, has to conclude that sovereign authority can never be dispersed, or diluted, in any way. Skinner explains this as a position which only ever commands:

> He [Bodin] is thus drawn by the logic of his own ideological commitment into arguing that in any political society there must be a sovereign who is absolute in the sense that he commands but is never commanded, and so can never be lawfully opposed by any of his subjects.[11]

If sovereignty is 'absolute and perpetual', then it cannot be dissolved in any way and only rests with the self-identical sovereign power itself. King John himself articulates, at times, just such a Bodin-like reliance on his own person as the source of his authority. So when, in the opening scene, John's authority is threatened by talk of his 'borrowed' majesty, he tells Châtillon to return to the French king with a message that defiantly produces his kingship as dependent on nothing but his own physical presence. He claims that it is from that unique and apparently inalienable presence that he derives his authority:

> Be thou as lightning in the eyes of France,
> For ere thou canst report, I will be there;
> The thunder of my cannon shall be heard. (1.1.24–6)

Relying on his own body to support claims to sovereign authority is something that John also does later on in the play but, by that point, his absolutist-type claims are revealed as unworkable. At the walls of his city, the besieged citizen of Angers asks how he should 'know the King' and he receives these two answers from the two candidates:

> KING PHILIPPE Know him in us, that here hold up his [Prince Arthur's] right.
> KING JOHN In us, that are our own great deputy
> And bear possession of our person here,
> Lord of our presence, Angers, and of you. (2.1.364–7)

King John contains, within himself, his own 'deputy'; sovereignty is not to be understood, so he claims in these instances, as structured through the series of substitutions and replacements through which the sovereign body might otherwise operate. John's sense of sovereign authority, at these moments, is that it is indivisible and exclusively embodied in his person. That is, with the phrase 'our person', he insists, *pace* Bodin, on there being no difference between his self-possessed body and the body of the king as an embodiment of the sovereign state.

But this is not how the action of the play works itself out at all. Already, King John's somewhat awkward phrase – 'our own great deputy' – might hint at a sovereignty that is not entirely inalienable from the 'person of the sovereign'. Moreover, the town of Angers that he is seeking to command rejects any innate claims to sovereign authority. The citizens refuse to admit that sovereignty is recognisable in the sense that John puts it to them: as an inalienable and instantly recognisable quality inherent to his possession of his own person. They decide, instead, to wait until the two kings have worked it out for themselves. They even refer to the two kings as the 'double majestie' (2.1.479), a phrase that is almost an oxymoron.

### Prosthesis, Sovereign Agency and the 'Hand'

It is, of course, no coincidence that *King John* contains more uses of the word 'hand' than any other of Shakespeare's plays. It is a play that is very much concerned with agency, with the capacity to act on your own behalf and, more notably, what it means to act in place of someone else; that is, to lend somebody a hand. One way into thinking about this non-agential hand would be to consider work already undertaken on the early modern hand, particularly in its relationship to writing. This work may, in turn, allow us to see the hand, in relation to sovereignty, as always a kind of prosthesis, always capable of being detached and disowned. So Jonathan Goldberg's account of the 'hand' in relation to 'character' in Shakespeare stresses the artifactual nature of character through a close examination of socially embedded practices of handwriting. In Shakespeare's use of 'hand' to mean a person's typical writing, or even signature, Goldberg writes that 'the hand, materialised, is emphatically a social hand, the disowned mark of material production'.[12] In *King John*, the hand is similarly construed in relation to sovereignty. That is, the 'hand' that works on behalf of sovereign power – whether to stab someone on the king's behalf or to hand over a crown – has no necessary relation to a single owner; it, too, is 'disowned'. Drawing, in part, on Goldberg's work, Anton Bosman sees something of this happening in Shakespeare's *All is True* wherein the traditional oral authority of the king and his deputies – in this play, Wolsey – is superseded, and preceded, by the king's 'hand' which, unlike oral testimony and its symbolic representation in the royal seal, is not, necessarily, underwritten by the presence of the king's body.[13] It is detachable; letters and documents are always in transit. And in any case, as work on the early modern secretary has pointed out, the 'hand' of the king, or of any prince or aristocrat, is more likely to be the work of a professional employee than that of the master himself.[14]

In his lectures on sovereignty, Derrida, like Skinner, privileges Bodin as the main source of the early modern idea of a sovereignty that is indivisible, calling him 'the first great theorist of political sovereignty'.[15] Bodin's assertion of a sovereignty that is inalienable should be considered an aspect of what Derrida refers to as sovereignty's '*ipseity*' ('self-ness') which he glosses as follows: 'The sovereign, in the broadest sense of the term, is he who has the right and the strength to be and be recognised as *himself, the same, properly the same as himself*.'[16] Kings may lay claim to a self-sustaining originality in their production of sovereign authority, the legitimacy of this located in the idea that their position is derived from God and/or inherited from the previous occupant of the throne. King John's phrase, quoted earlier – 'our own great deputy' – certainly complicates this picture, but any such Bodin-like assertions of self-similitude are, in any case, always in the process of breaking up. As Derrida says elsewhere in these seminars, sovereignty is only ever '*said* to be indivisible – said and supposed to be indivisible but always divisible'.[17] This does seem to contradict statements from earlier in the seminars where he puts it that 'divisible or sharable sovereignty is not sovereignty'.[18] Jacques Lezra describes this apparent contradiction as Derrida's 'two-step project' in which he is 'describing and displacing the "integral sovereignty" on which sovereignty turns'.[19] Here, then, Derrida would read the relationship between Bodin and Hobbes quite differently from Skinner. Rather than grounding them in the ongoing legitimisation of the authoritarian nation-state, Derrida points towards their distinctive figurations of the supposed self-sufficiency of the sovereign. He outlines the peculiar and monstrous 'animal-machine' of Hobbes's *Leviathan*, associating it with the word 'prosthstatic': a sovereignty that claims 'exception' in the way that Bodin uses the term, but is nevertheless sustained by prosthetic attachment. Some of Shakespeare's imagery around the sovereign prefigures these Hobbesian 'prosthstatics'.

Derrida's 'two-step project' might also be a way of thinking about how, in *King John*, claims to a stable sovereignty, embodied in the 'person' of the king, are never secure. The transactional nature of sovereign power, seen in Shakespeare's plays, interrogates the relationship between '*ipseity*' and the 'prosthstatic', between a drive to locate sovereignty in the person of the king and representations of sovereignty that see it dispersed. Bodin's conception of sovereignty as 'unique' or self-sustaining, rather than supplementary and transactional ('prosthstatic'), is, I suggest, called into question by *King John*'s synecdochal 'hand' and its accompanying investigations of agency. Derrida's sense of sovereignty's claims to '*ipseity*' as only ever apparently the case is played out through this play's concern with the difficulties of acting in place of the king. As the Derridean neologism indicates, 'prosthesis' could also figure this entanglement of bodies and body parts, within the effects of sovereignty; it might also describe some of the peculiarities of sovereign agency as always already 'borrowed', attenuated in some way. If synecdoche produces its meanings and effects through constant shifts between the literal and the figurative (the somatic and the symbolic, the incorporated and the cut-off), then the figure of synecdoche should be thought of as having a significant relationship with the idea of prosthesis, which similarly shifts between the incorporated and the dislocated. 'Prosthesis', David Wills writes, assumes 'reciprocity between word and body'.[20] In locking the body into a relationship with technology, prosthesis renders indistinct any straightforward understanding of what lies inside, and what lies outside, the body. Alongside this, other categorisations are also blurred:

> 'Prosthesis' necessarily refers to two contradictory but complementary operations: amputation and addition; and then, of course, the animal and mineral, living or natural and artificial, and so on. There is nothing that is simply or singularly prosthetic; it has no originary integrality.[21]

Why this is useful as a description of some aspects of sovereignty is that it interrogates agency in the synecdochal relations of sovereignty. What is available in the particular relationship that synecdoche has with sovereignty is an understanding of the sovereign state as itself prosthetic, as itself having 'no originary integrality'. What we see is that it is formed, rather, through a confutation of 'amputation' with 'addition'; detachment from, and incorporation within, the 'body politic' are both at stake in sovereign relations.

In many Shakespearean descriptions of sovereign majesty, sovereignty is conceived of through a collection of prosthetic attachments, rather than through the, perhaps more expected, relations of sovereignty and divinity, or sovereignty and blood. It is an example probably written by Thomas Nashe, however, for *The First Part of Henry Sixth*, that provides an extraordinary occasion for representing and investigating this 'prosthetic' kind of sovereignty. The play opens with the funeral of Henry V, and with the coffin of the dead king being carried across the stage. Kantorowicz argues for the historical importance of Henry's actual funeral effigy, on display over his coffin in France, as an event that helped spread the English custom of the royal funeral effigy to the French royal family, so that when Charles VI died shortly afterwards, he became the first French king also to have an effigy.[22] Some memory of that effigy, or of its effects, might be seen and heard to linger in the opening scene of this play, even though it is apparently not brought in with the coffin. Gloucester's blazon of the dead Henry V's various attributes, spoken over his displayed coffin, certainly produces him as a work of prosthesis, blending the organic with the technological:

> England ne'er had a king until his time.
> Virtue he had, deserving to command.
> His brandished sword did blind men with his beams.
> His arms spread wider than a dragon's wings.
> His sparkling eyes, replete with wrathful fire,
> More dazzled and drove back his enemies
> Than midday sun, fierce bent against their faces. (1.1.8–14)

This anatomy of sovereign authority by means of the figure of blazon delineates sovereignty through its prosthetic attachments, both organic and inorganic: blinding swords and blazing eyes, and arms that are impossibly wide, dragons' wings being notoriously immeasurable. Gloucester's speech continues with a further figure of the impossibility of expression (*adynaton*): 'What should I say? His deeds exceed all speech. / He ne'er lift up his hand but conquerèd' (1.1.15–16). Itself almost detached from, or prosthetically attached to, the main blazon, the phrase 'lift up his hand' has particular implications for the agency of sovereign authority. This hand seems briefly detachable in the list-like aspects of the blazon: both part of Henry's sovereign will, something that acts, but also something that is acted *upon*, lifted up and, therefore, separable. Prosthesis, particularly the prosthetic hand, is, like the use of synecdoche, a concept that provides for a consideration of the notion of agency. Shakespeare's blazon does not produce a static image of excepted sovereign authority so much as a version of sovereignty that can only truly emerge in movement, in the lifting up of a hand with a weapon in it.

In *King John*, as we have seen, the sword is the first symbol of sovereignty that is imagined as being passed from hand to hand, out of the hand of the supposed usurper, John, and into the hands of the legitimate Prince Arthur. Much later, in the final act of the play, during the odd scene of John's second coronation, the crown itself is passed from hand to hand, from King John to the Pope's legate, Pandolf, and back again:

> KING JOHN [*giving Pandolf his crown*]
> Thus have I yielded up into your *hand*
> The circle of my glory.
> PANDOLF [*returning the crown*] Take again
> From this my *hand*, as holding of the Pope,
> Your sovereign greatness and authority. (5.1.1–4; my emphases and stage
>   directions)

The paired gestures of the two actors playing the king and Pandolf, and the to-ing and fro-ing of the crown as a stage property, undermine the usually intended significance of a coronation: the investment of timeless sovereign authority in the body of *this* king here and now. Here, instead, the provisional and transactional nature of this investment is emphasised, lending weight to the earlier claims of the English nobility that this second coronation is 'superfluous' (4.2.4) and that this 'double pomp' (9) is 'wasteful and ridiculous excess' (16). It is awkwardly supplementary. It obfuscates any indication of divine origin for Pandolf's capacity to invest sovereignty in the person of King John. Jean Howard and Phyllis Rackin claim that this double coronation ensures that 'Everything, even the unique ceremony by which monarchical authority is passed down in temporal succession from one male ruler to the next, now becomes repeatable and reversible.'[23] Barbara Traister points out something similar when she argues that 'John's own lack of belief in what should be his ceremonious second body becomes clear to the audience as well as to his nobles when he chooses to be crowned a second time.'[24] Furthermore, by the time we get to this point in the play, this word 'hand', foregrounded for the last time in this scene, has become so overdetermined through repeated use, and by its association with conflicting accounts of sovereign power, that the scene and its gestures are unavoidably ironic. The 'hand' that transfers sovereignty here produces that sovereignty as always supplemental: as Derridean 'prosthstatics' rather than self-possessed; as already 'borrowed' rather than ever securely the possession of one body.

## Hands in *King John*: Hubert and Prince Arthur

References to the 'hand' in *King John* are concentrated in two related episodes: the king's dealings with his agent, Hubert, and the aftermath of the death of Prince Arthur. These two parts of the play feature multiple and contested uses of the word 'hand'. In the king's conversations with Hubert, a significant question emerges over the extent to which the deputy can be held responsible for his own actions and, contrariwise, the extent to which his actions can be thought of as distinguishable from the intentions of the king. In his actions, does he 'borrow' any of the king's 'majesty'? This is part of the play's continued interest in forms of secondariness, running from the 'borrowed majesty' of the opening lines to the doubled image of sovereignty at the end of the play: the corpse of King John being wept over by his heir, Prince Henry, an iconic image of the immortality of the crown that is nevertheless pervaded by mourning, disease and death. The oddly comic episode of Falconbridge and the Bastard in the opening scene also interrupts the concept of an innate sovereignty with accounts of doubling and imperfect replication, as the true lineaments of the Plantaganet line are rediscovered in the archetypal figure of illegitimate inauthenticity, the comic stage 'bastard'.

In Act 4, scene 2 of the play, King John confronts Hubert, believing that he has followed his orders and killed the imprisoned Prince Arthur, the French-sponsored claimant to the English throne. Since asking Hubert to kill Arthur, the king has changed his mind. The English nobility instead require that he release the young prince as their price for supporting his imperilled reign. Hubert has not, in fact, obeyed John and killed the prince, but until this point he pretends that he has, so as not to anger the king. Prince Arthur does, however, die, as we discover in the play's following scene when he throws himself off a wall, which he does at the same time as expressing the hope that this act will not in fact lead to his death. This outline of the plot already points towards complex networks of agency and responsibility. Who it is that actually kills Arthur is an open question. In the interactions between John and Hubert, the implications of this for sovereign agency are drawn out through a focus on the 'hand':

> KING JOHN Thy hand hath murdered him. I had a mighty cause
> To wish him dead, but thou hadst none to kill him. (4.2.204–5)

John, despite saying that he had wished Arthur dead, claims (disingenuously of course) that the responsibility lies solely with the hand that actually wielded the knife. The king's implication is that this hand is Hubert's and his alone, the hand as a straightforward synecdoche for the individual will, intentions and actions of the supposed killer. Hubert, however, refuses to accept sole responsibility for an action that, in fact, he has not even been able to undertake, his conscience not allowing him. He gives John at least some of the blame, locating the burden of responsibility for this act on the relations of sovereignty itself: 'My hand, my Lord? Why, did you not provoke me?' (4.2.208).[25] John claims, at this point, to be a misunderstood king, who cannot be held responsible for those people who act on his behalf. Hubert counters this by redefining John's use of the word 'hand', and by introducing another way of understanding it: 'Here is your hand and seal for what I did' (4.2.214). The 'hand' of the king has, apparently, signed a warrant. John briefly entertains this, deploying the royal 'we' and admitting that this is 'Witness against us to damnation' (4.2.217). But then, through further uses and redefinitions of 'hand', he seeks again to reassign responsibility for the murder in such a way as almost to anonymise the act: it is nature's 'hand', nature's fault:

> How oft the sight of means to do ill deeds,
> Make deeds ill done! Hadst not thou been by,
> A fellow by the *hand* of nature marked,
> Quoted, and signed to do a deed of shame,
> This murder had not come into my mind. (4.2.220–4; my emphasis)

King John's problem has gone from one in which his agent, Hubert, has acted too much on his own, to his bearing an uncanny proximity to his own will:

> Hadst thou but shook thy head or made a pause
> When I spake darkly what I purposèd,
> Or turned an eye of doubt upon my face,
> As bid me tell my tale in express words,
> Deep shame had struck me dumb, made me break off,
> And those thy fears might have wrought fears in me.
> But thou didst understand me by my signs,
> And didst in signs again parley with sin;
> Yea, without stop, didst let thy heart consent,
> And consequently thy rude hand to act
> The deed which both our tongues held vile to name. (4.2.232–42)

It is interesting that, at this point, the king glosses Hubert's hand as 'rude', a word that elsewhere in Shakespeare has associations with the merely mechanical, or the basely material (for example, the 'rude mechanicals' of *A Midsummer Night's Dream*). I take it that, here, the king is implying that no sovereign intent or will of his own can lie behind Hubert's hand. But this is precisely what is under dispute: the extent to which any action that Hubert takes is his own, or the king's, responsibility. The other owner of 'rude hands' in the history plays is the 'irregular and wild' Glendower, described in Westmorland's narration of Mortimer's capture at the start of *Henry IV* part one (1.1.40–1). Here, Westmorland's description of Glendower merges with his description of the 'beastly transformation' enacted by the 'Welshwomen' on the corpses of the noble English dead. Again, the suggestion is of a hand that cannot be referred back to the distinct propriety of a sovereign will. Elsewhere in *King John*, 'rude' (which, like 'hand', appears more frequently in *King John* than in any other play) is used to suggest the chaos upon which sovereign order is required to act. In the final scene, as the dying King John is brought in, the young Prince Henry is told, 'Be of good comfort Prince, for you are born / To set a form upon that indigest / Which he hath left so shapeless and so rude' (5.7.25–7). While the suggestion from Salisbury might be one of a coherent transfer of power from one king to another, the onstage spectacle of the raving King John, who dies pronouncing, 'all this thou seest is but a clod / And module of confounded royalty' (5.7.57–8) gives the lie to Salisbury's optimism.

In this scene, Hubert eventually comes clean and admits that he did not murder Prince Arthur. But King John's idea of an order that remained unheard and unspoken does echo the peculiar manner in which Hubert was first instructed – if 'instructed' is the word – to kill Arthur, in an earlier scene. There, Hubert says that he is 'much bounden' to his king, to which John replies:

> Good friend, thou hast no cause to say so yet,
> But thou shalt have; and creep time ne'er so slow,
> Yet it shall come for me to do thee good.
> I had a thing to say – but let it go. (3.3.30–3)

John's coyness about his intentions continues with the following still more peculiar suggestions, which translate his instructions into something like an intimate telepathy:

> Or if thou couldst see me without eyes,
> Hear me without thine ears, and make reply
> Without a tongue, using conceit alone,
> Without eyes, ears, and harmful sound of words;
> Then, in despite of broad-eyed watchful day
> I would into thy bosom pour my thoughts.
> But, ah, I will not. Yet I love thee well,
> And by my troth, I think thou lov'st me well. (3.3.48–55)

This reluctance to speak his will ('without a tongue') is completely different from the mode of kingship that John has deployed earlier in the play. Where this had been a mode that seemed to rely upon presence and on an active agency, associated with his voice being heard, and defined against a French mode of kingship that is structured through secondary agents and substitutes, he now attempts something quite different. He is trying to get Hubert to act on his behalf but in a way that cannot tie the consequences of that action – the murder – to his own sovereign will. Less fastidious about his reputation, Richard III, when he wants the two young princes to be killed in the Tower of London, nevertheless does begin in a similarly circumspect vein, as he hints to Buckingham, 'Young Edward lives. Think what I speak' (4.2.11), and continues, 'Ha? Am I king? 'Tis so. But Edward lives' (4.2.15). Whether Buckingham is feigning ignorance of Richard's intentions or not, he seems not to get the message, and the newly minted king gives up: 'Shall I be plain? I want the bastards dead, / And I would have it immediately performed' (4.2.19–20).

Some of Elizabeth I's rhetoric in public speeches preceding the execution of Mary, Queen of Scots, makes similarly interesting use of these ambiguities related to agency and responsibility. The conflict between Hubert and John over the responsibility for the death of Prince Arthur was, in the days of the old historicism, given precise allegorical links to the circumstances surrounding the execution of Mary, Queen of Scots, in particular seeing Hubert as a parallel for William Davidson, the private secretary given responsibility for conveying the death warrant, who was later imprisoned by Elizabeth for misinterpreting her wishes. Without necessarily wanting to revive this allegorical reading of historical parallels, nor to dismiss this particular connection as entirely inappropriate, these contexts are highly suggestive. However, as I say, I believe it is not just in Elizabeth's reaction to the eventual execution of Mary, but also in her rhetoric in public speeches preceding the execution that we might see the crucial context for this episode.[26]

In this scene, the intimate telepathy that King John attempts to bring into play in his relationship with his agent, Hubert, is something that Elizabeth I also seems to suggest in her speeches to parliament. In 1586 she made two speeches in response to parliament's petition in favour of executing Mary. It is the tortured rhetoric of the closing to the second speech that can most be likened to John's mystification of responsibility in *King John*:

> But now for answer unto you, you must take an answer without answer at my hands. For if I should say I would not do it, I should peradventure say that which I did not think, and otherwise than it might be. If I should say that I would do it, it were not fit in this place and at this time, although I did mean it. Wherefore I must desire you to hold yourselves satisfied with this answer answerless. I know there is none of you but is wise and well affected towards me and therefore will consider what is most fit for me to do. There must be deeds and not words which must satisfice your demand.[27]

I take the message of both of Elizabeth's speeches to parliament on this matter to be fairly clear. While she has every reason to wish Mary dead, she needs it not to be her responsibility. Ideally, Mary's death would simply take place. As in *King John*, Elizabeth invokes a kind of telepathy whereby her subjects are encouraged to operate on her behalf, but only in her absence. In a sense, this is what happens in the play when, in the emblematic central scene, Prince Arthur throws himself off his prison walls. He hopes that this will not kill him but as he dies, he claims that the rocks on to which he has fallen have somehow taken on the sovereign will of the king: 'O me, my uncle's spirit lies in these stones' (4.3.9).

In fact, his is a death that occurs to the benefit of all the protagonists in the play. The French have, at this point, already decided that they would rather be rid of him in favour of the Dauphin as their new rival to King John for the English crown. This boy's abject body, lying broken on the rocks – lying there, in fact, for some time in the ensuing scene before anyone notices it – is caught up within the typical workings of sovereignty. The play focuses on Arthur's abject body and places it centre stage, and it does this in various ways, both in the fact that it lies there with nobody mentioning it – in its centrality in the plot – and then in the fact that the play ends with the advancement of another young prince, Prince Henry, whose emergence announces a somewhat hollow expectation that England has been rescued through the violence and corruption that the play traces throughout the narrative proper.

When the corpse of Prince Arthur is finally noticed, described movingly as 'this ruin of sweet life' (4.3.65), the use of synecdochal 'hands', as in the scenes with Hubert, foregrounds the questions of accountability that the seemingly agentless death of Arthur might have worked to mystify:

> BASTARD [*on discovering Prince Arthur's body*]
> It is a damnèd, and a bloody work;
> The graceless action of a heavy *hand* –
> If that it be the work of any *hand*.
> SALISBURY If that it be the work of any *hand*?
> We had a kind of light, what would ensue:
> It is the shameful work of Hubert's *hand*,
> The practice, and the purpose of the King;
> From whose obedience I forbid my soul,
> Kneeling before this ruin of sweet life,
> And breathing to this breathless excellence
> The incense of a vow, a holy vow,
> Never to taste the pleasures of the world,
> Never to be infected with delight,
> Nor conversant with ease and idleness,
> Till I have set a glory to this *hand*,
> By giving it the worship of revenge. (4.3.57–72; my emphases and stage direction)

The Bastard, here as promoter of this 'answer answerless'/'speechless speech' version of unaccountable sovereignty and untraceable sovereign violence, introduces the possibility that this was not the work of any hand, but that it, somehow, just happened. Salisbury refuses to countenance this and insists on the joint culpability of Hubert and the king. Hubert's hand, in Salisbury's version, is not his own but acts as a substitute for the wilful intentions of the king himself. He reinserts agency into the act. The ironies of this, however, are multiple. In one sense, although the play makes no distinct claim that he is committing suicide, Arthur did die at his own hands and Hubert did not enact the king's will. But that is not to say that the king did not actively will the boy's death and put in place the process to ensure that it happened. That Salisbury and Pembroke use this as grounds to defect to the French side renders it more complex. It could be seen by an English audience as an act of treason, and these historical figures were often held up as types of the wicked traitor. Yet they, themselves, become potential victims of sovereign violence, as the French prepare to murder them once they have outlived their usefulness.

Hubert's and John's multifariously figured hands throughout these extended episodes – episodes that are crucial to the security of John's kingship – reveal any claims to an inalienable sovereignty, secured in the person of the king, to be unsustainable. Sovereignty, as elsewhere in Shakespeare's histories, is only fleetingly possessed, available in transaction rather than permanently secured in the person of a king. And Shakespeare's use of synecdochal body parts interrogates these processes of possession and dispossession, and of sovereign will and deputisation.

## A Succession of Bastards: Shakespearean Sovereignty

*King John* ends with an image of sovereignty that might superficially seem to echo the theory of the 'king's two bodies' that has, since Kantorowicz, been associated both with Shakespeare's history plays and the medieval inheritances of the Tudor state, and which has, more recently, been at the heart of a renewed interest in Shakespearean sovereignties, particularly as they relate to political theology. Once King John has died on stage, King Henry (Henry III) weeps over his father's corpse: a visual equivalent to the perennial phrase, 'The King is dead; long live the King'. In recent years, the precise relevance of the theory of the king's two bodies as a concept through which Elizabethan sovereignty might be understood and that, by extension, might be in operation in the history plays has been thrown into doubt. Lorna Hutson's argument, for example, as outlined in the Introduction, reveals the idea of the 'king's two bodies' to be little more than a legal fiction. Tracing this counter-influence through the history plays, Hutson argues that where, in *Richard II*, the monarch does start out by 'pretending to the position of the judge', this is ultimately confounded in the subsequent action of the play and its sequels, and that, by the end of *Henry IV* part two, the monarch admits his status as dependent on the law. She quotes, in support of this conclusion, Prince Harry (Henry V), speaking to the Lord Chief Justice who had earlier had him arrested for his lawless behaviour:

> You did commit me,
> For which I do commit into your hand
> Th'unstainèd sword that you have used to bear,
> With this remembrance: that you use the same
> With the like bold, just, and impartial spirit
> As you have done 'gainst me. There is my hand. (5.2.111–16)

Hands again, transacting sovereignty. Hutson is surely right that this is a potentially 'subversive' set of ideas if they are imagined as countermanding absolutist understandings of sovereign authority.[28] Henry V is conceding that, in part and at times, sovereignty can be somewhere other than contained in his person and that it can, in fact, be moved from 'hand' to 'hand'.

What is at stake in the final scene of *King John* is not the uncomplicated restatement of political theology that might underwrite an absolutist theory of sovereignty: an eternal sovereignty transferred from dead king to living son. The transfers of sovereign authority that these plays are really interested in are not always a question of heredity at all but are more to do with deputising; they are fragmentary, synecdochal and syntagmatic rather than paradigmatic images of unity. The last words of *King John* are not those of Henry III, mourning his dead father, but of the Bastard:

> This England never did, nor never shall,
> Lie at the proud foot of a conqueror
> But when it first did help to wound itself.
> Now these her princes are come home again,
> Come the three corners of the world in arms
> And we shall shock them. Naught shall make us rue
> If England to itself do rest but true. (5.7.112–18)

The Bastard, himself, is a fascinatingly synecdochal – even prosthetic – figure, whose body is, and is not, part of the royal succession.[29] His position in this scene, mediating true succession, serves only to highlight the bastardisation of all sovereign transactions, from one hand to another. Deputation or succession: what's the difference? In this speech, England's eternal sovereignty, whatever the gung-ho spirit in which the Bastard speaks here, is radically displaced from the body of the monarch. Civil conflict, as the Bastard imagines England to 'wound itself', is resolved not in the person of the sovereign but, first, in multiple 'princes' and then in a 'we': an England that has the opportunity to remain somehow 'true' to itself. It is not Henry III who comes into being over the corpse of King John, but something that looks a little like the anonymous nation-state, with sovereign power disbursed through multiple agencies.

Despite the onstage spectacle that apparently reproduces the king's 'two bodies', this is, then, a long way from Kantorowicz's version of political theology, or from the production of the king's body as in any way a sacred repository of sovereignty. One of the most trenchant applications of theories of political theology to the history plays has been Ken Jackson's argument that *King John* 'illuminates and supports the historical accuracy' of Agamben's delineations of sovereignty in relation to the body in *Homo Sacer*. He concludes this discussion by seeing, in Prince Arthur, a type of 'bare life', a body 'that remains inaccessible to the juridical-political order'.[30] This is a compelling argument, given the pathos with which the spectacle of the dead prince is delineated. But what I have been arguing is that, rather than locating the relationship between the body and sovereign power in structures of exception, whether Bodinesque 'majesty' or extra-legal 'bare life', Shakespeare repeatedly focuses attention, in this play and elsewhere, on the problems of political agency and does this through figurations of the body that refute any notion of bodily self-possession. This is not quite the same thing as thinking sovereignty through 'bare life' in the manner of, say, Daniel Juan Gil's 'anti-politics'. Such a reification of the body as a site that escapes inclusion in the public realm (whether through sovereign exception or through reduction to 'bare life') and that, therefore, offers a redemption from politics is not something that is always supported by an examination of the ways that bodies are represented in the history plays. Body parts – hands in *King John* – in Shakespeare's history plays are always, through varying modes of representation including metaphor, metonymy and the act of personation itself, articulated in relation either to each other or to objects (weapons; letters; symbols of state power such as crowns, orbs, swords).

What *King John* is interested in, and what much of its action demonstrates, are the problems attendant on these self-divided, prosthetic, sovereign forms. This is a form of political theory, rather than a political theology. Bradin Cormack has written about Bodin's version of a sovereignty that has to remain inalienable, claiming that this theory, in the end, 'erodes sovereignty from within, by intensifying its vulnerability to the differences it is unable properly to acknowledge'.[31] These 'differences' do, however, emerge in Shakespeare's more transactional notion of sovereignty. *King John*, the play, is an extended acknowledgement of these differences within sovereignty that 'erode' it 'from within'.

The problems for political agency that this entails (to what extent is it possible to act on behalf of, or in the place of, a sovereign power?) can also be seen, later in the period, in some aspects of Hobbes, and specifically in an example that Hobbes provides that echoes the problems set out for Hubert in *King John*. At one point in *Leviathan*, Hobbes argues that the subject is not always obliged to obey the commands of the sovereign, and that the subject retains some residual independence from the prosthetic ('prosthstatic') sovereign state. There is, for Hobbes, a 'natural Liberty' which resists incorporation into the sovereign state:

> Again, the Consent of a Subject to Sovereaign Power, is contained in these words, *I Authorise, or take upon me, all his actions*; in which there is no restriction at all, of his own former natural Liberty: For by allowing him to *kill me*, I am not bound to kill my self when he commands me. 'Tis one thing to say, *I will kill my selfe, or my fellow*.[32]

He concludes, from this, that 'No man is bound . . . either to kill himself, or any other man.'[33] The exception to this would be if the subject were ordered to kill someone and the purpose of the order were to further the 'End for which the Soveraignty was ordained'. Then, we would have 'no Liberty to refuse'.[34] The difficulty of Hobbes's argument here articulates a potentially circular logic in which, momentarily, a subject (a deputised agent such as Hubert, perhaps) is placed in the position of being the judge of the validity of a sovereign's actions. In this exemplary moment, when a king is charging somebody to undertake a potentially illegal killing, Hobbes considers that the subject is momentarily detached from the sovereign state in order to judge the extent of her own incorporation.

This is exactly the position that Hubert is in when asked by King John to kill Prince Arthur. In those scenes in which the king insinuates that he wants this to happen but subsequently claims that his intentions have been misinterpreted and even that a warrant sealed with his own 'hand' cannot be used as a reliable determinant of his sovereign will, the play relentlessly focuses our attention on the enduring conundrum of sovereign authority: what does it mean to act on behalf of sovereign authority? If I kill for a king, is it my responsibility or his? The play unravels these knotty questions through asking us repeatedly to consider what it means to have a 'hand' in something. The vision of sovereign power that results from this investigation does not see it hypostasised in the eternal presence of a crowned monarch. Rather, Shakespeare's versions of sovereign power see it as constantly shifting, moved from hand to hand through a succession of compromised transactions.

## Notes

1. David Wills, *Prosthesis* (Stanford: Stanford University Press, 1995), p. 45.
2. The joint runners-up for third place, with twenty-six apiece, are *Henry*

V and *Julius Caesar*, plays which share with *King John* a concern with personal responsibility for political action.
3. Farah Karim Cooper, *The Hand on the Shakespearean Stage: Gesture, Touch, and the Spectacle of Dismemberment* (London: Bloomsbury, 2016), p. 3.
4. Hillman and Mazzio, 'Introduction', pp. xiii–xiv.
5. George Puttenham, *The Arte of English Poesie* (London, 1589), sig. Y4r.
6. Cicero, *On the Ideal Orator [de Oratore]*, trans. James M. May and Jakob Wisse (Oxford: Oxford University Press, 2001), p. 274.
7. Puttenham, *The Arte of English Poesie*, sig. Y4r.
8. Ken Jackson, in an article on the relationship between *King John* and Agamben's *Homo Sacer*, also sees this opening scene as determining the play's concern with disputed sovereignty, claiming that *King John* is noteworthy, among Shakespeare's history plays, for 'how quickly and directly it addresses the problem of sovereign legitimacy'; Ken Jackson, '"Is It God or the Sovereign Exception?": Giorgio Agamben's *Homo Sacer* and Shakespeare's *King John*', *Literature and Religion* 38.3 (2006), p. 85.
9. Bodin, *On Sovereignty*, p. 1.
10. Bodin, *On Sovereignty*, p. 86.
11. Skinner, *The Foundations of Modern Political Thought*, vol. 2, p. 287.
12. Jonathan Goldberg, *Hamlet's Hand* (Minneapolis: University of Minnesota Press, 2002), p. 107. See also his book, *Writing Matter: From the Hands of the English Renaissance* (Stanford: Stanford University Press, 1991).
13. Anton Bosman, 'Seeing Tears: Truth and Sense in *All is True*', *Shakespeare Quarterly* 50.4 (1999), 465.
14. In addition to Goldberg's *Writing Matter*, see Richard Rambuss, *Spenser's Secret Career* (Cambridge: Cambridge University Press, 1993); and Katherine Rowe, *Dead Hands: Fictions of Agency: Renaissance to Modern* (Stanford: Stanford University Press, 2000). Rowe highlights these difficult questions of agency as emerging alongside an interest, in the early modern period, in disembodied hands. She discusses the case of John Stubbs, whose hand was judicially amputated for publishing the tract, *The Discoverie of a Gaping Gulf Where Into England is Like to be Swallowed by another French Marriage*, in which he had advised the Queen, at the height of the revival of the idea that she might marry the Duc d'Alencon, that she shouldn't. Stubbs is said to have come out with an appalling pun on the scaffold, 'Pray for me now my calamity is at hand.' After the amputation, he raised his hat with his one remaining (left) hand and declared, 'God Save the Queen', before fainting. *John Stubbs's Gaping Gulf with Letters and Other Relevant Documents*, ed. Lloyd E. Berry (Charlottesville: University Press of Virginia, 1970), p. xxxvi. Rowe naturally relates this to Shakespeare's *Titus Andronicus*, where similar plays are made around the symbolic and material nature of the severed hand and in which severed hands become a part of the plot. Of this play, she writes, 'In *Titus Andronicus*, to have a hand is to possess the sign and instrument of agency only tenuously and temporarily' (Rowe, *Dead Hands*, p. 286). That is, it is always possible that your hands are not, in fact, your own to hold on to.
15. Derrida, *The Beast and the Sovereign*, vol. I, p. 27.
16. Derrida, *The Beast and the Sovereign*, vol. I, p. 66.

17. Derrida, *The Beast and the Sovereign*, vol. I, p. 291.
18. Derrida, *The Beast and the Sovereign*, vol. I, p. 46
19. Lezra, *Wild Materialism*, p. 64.
20. Wills, *Prosthesis*, p. 143.
21. Wills, *Prosthesis*, p. 133.
22. Kantorowicz, *The King's Two Bodies*, p. 421.
23. Jean E. Howard and Phyllis Rackin, *Engendering a Nation: A Feminist Account of Shakespeare's English Histories* (London: Routledge, 1997), p. 132.
24. Barbara Traister, 'The King's One Body: Unceremonial Kingship in *King John*', in Deborah Curren-Aquino (ed.), *King John: New Perspectives* (Newark: University of Delaware Press, 1989), p. 93.
25. The Oxford editors have amended the original here, which reads, 'No had my lord …' The word, 'had' in the original is rather odd and, even though there is no explicit textual evidence to support the change that they have made, it does make sense.
26. See Lily Campbell, 'Shakespeare's Histories: Mirrors of Elizabethan Policy', *The American Historical Review* 52.4 (1947), pp. 725–7; and E. A. J. Honigman, 'Introduction', *King John* (2nd Arden edn) (London: Methuen, 1954).
27. Elizabeth I, *Collected Works*, ed. Leah S. Marcus, Janel Mueller and Mary Beth Rose (Chicago: University of Chicago Press, 2000), pp. 199–200.
28. For other dissenting accounts of the influence of 'political theology', see David Norbrook, 'The Emperor's New Body? *Richard II*, Ernst Kantorowicz, and the Politics of Shakespeare Criticism', *Textual Practice* 10 (1996), pp. 329–57; and Victoria Kahn, 'Political Theology and Fiction in *The King's Two Bodies*', *Representations* 106 (2009), pp. 77–101.
29. For discussions of the play which centre on the Bastard as a representative of new forms of political behaviour, see Thomas Anderson, '"Legitimation, name, and all is gone": Bastardy and Bureaucracy in Shakespeare's *King John*', *Journal for Early Modern Cultural Studies* 4 (2004), pp. 35–61; and Edward Gieskes, '"He is but a Bastard to the Time": Status and Service in *The Troublesome Raigne of John* and Shakespeare's *King John*', *ELH* 65 (1998), pp. 779–98.
30. Jackson, '"Is It God or the Sovereign Exception?"', p. 97.
31. Bradin Cormack, 'Shakespeare's Other Sovereignty: on Particularity and Violence in *The Winter's Tale* and the Sonnets', *Shakespeare Quarterly* 62.4 (2011), p. 491.
32. Thomas Hobbes, *Leviathan*, ed. C. B. McPherson (Harmondsworth: Penguin, 1968), p. 269.
33. Hobbes, *Leviathan*, p. 269.
34. Hobbes, *Leviathan*, p. 269.

# Chapter 4

# Copious Sovereignty in the *Henry IV* Plays

PRINCE Wilt thou rob this leathern-jerkin, crystal-button, knot-pated, agate-ring, puke-stocking, caddis-garter, smooth-tongue, Spanish-pouch?
FRANCIS O Lord, sir, who do you mean? (*Henry IV* part one, 2.5.58–61)

Shakespeare did not need to write a second *Henry IV* play because the complexity of the plot demanded it. Part two really just repeats the narrative of part one, albeit with a slightly different set of rebels and with a king who is now even sicker, closer to death, and seemingly even more compromised by his own path to power. Neither are the two parts needed to fulfil any demand for a balanced pair of tetralogies; the plays did not exist as a set of eight plays until the *Henry VI* plays were placed in chronological order in the 1623 Folio. Rather, Shakespeare needs two *Henry IV* plays because one would not have been enough to contain the vast amount of words that he seems, in these plays in particular, to be intent on using. Nicholas Crawford describes the two plays as 'this curious swollen center of the *Henriad*'.[1] Shakespeare's writing is always dilatory, but it becomes so copious, so 'swollen', in the *Henry IV* plays that there would never be enough room in just one play to contain all the lists, similes, metaphors, analogies and hyperbole that occupy him throughout the dialogue. Moreover, the process of rewriting *Henry IV* part two, as outlined in the Introduction, extended the figurative language of the quarto text well beyond a capacity merely to signify. That impulse to dilate signification through proliferating figuration, evident in almost all of Shakespeare's writing, is taken to almost caricatured lengths in the two *Henry IV* plays. These two plays are, if nothing else, an exercise in the rhetorical practice of *copia* and, also, an investigation into the relation of this figure of speech to disorder. That there are two parts to *Henry IV* merely further establishes the commitment to *copia* that is evident everywhere in these plays; the plays are multiply, almost pointlessly, copious. Echoing Patricia Parker's identification of a fixation on 'doubling' in the two plays, Crawford maintains that this results in a steady 'dilution' of any original plenitude. If *copia*, he writes, is 'a kind of increase and elaboration', it is also 'a form of dilution'.[2]

*Copia*, as the basis for written and verbal expression, is the archetypal figure of Renaissance eloquence, but it is also a form that always risks spiralling out of control. Robert Grudin claims that to think in terms of the rhetorical figure of *copia*

> is to abandon certainty, to recognise previously unadmitted attractions or antipathies to people and pursuits, to question the authority of established truths and reigning idols, to account for unexplained anxieties, to face darkness and the unknown, to dissolve one's own identity into an ocean of diverse experience.[3]

The humanist tradition, stemming from Erasmus's theorisations of *copia* and his use of *copia* in texts such as his *Praise of Folly*, breaks down in Shakespeare's use. If, in an ideal form, *copia* is intended, as Grudin puts it, 'to appreciate a subject from every possible perspective, to make a tour of the interpretive means', thereby to come to a fuller understanding of a topic, then this is not really how it works in the *Henry IV* plays, where meaning is, rather, exhausted through obsessive extrapolations.[4] Grudin goes on to argue that *copia* is at its best when its particular imaginative energies are combined with 'rigorous thought, exacting, and self-critical'.[5] This is precisely what does not happen in the *Henry IV* plays which are, rather, suffused with forms of *copia* that are boundlessly labyrinthine. The capacity for *copia* to spin out of control and to dissipate rather than secure meaning – even in Erasmus's formulations – is acknowledged by Terence Cave. Erasmus, he tells us, warns against the specious overuse of copiousness in language, untethered from particular purpose, but the links that Erasmus begins to make between generative language and the metamorphoses of nature can readily outstrip language's capacity for order:

> The centrifugal movement which constantly asserts and reasserts itself throughout the *de Copia* and its prolific successors, that same movement of discourse towards pleasure, towards a place of celebration which is also a place of fiction, triumphs in spite of Erasmus's cautions.[6]

Jeffrey Yu shows that in *Julius Caesar*, a play that also draws some of its rhetorical energies from uses of *copia*, Shakespeare produces a world of political uncertainty and misinterpretation. That play, Yu argues, dramatises the ambiguities of interpretation that are inherent both in the narrative of authoritarianism and of rebellion – 'the ambiguous and contradictory Caesar of Renaissance tradition' – that is a feature of the play and that is also made available in the semantically generative capacities of *copia*.[7] In the *Henry IV* plays, however, the generative capacities of *copia* take a much darker turn, linking images of diseased and damaged bodies to a 'centrifugal movement' away from centres of sovereign power that is both geographical and political. *Copia*, in the plays, is further linked to forms of cataloguing, to 'reckonings' and to accounts that never tally. I identified a lack, or failure, of equivalences as characteristic of the way that sovereign power is imagined in *Henry V*. This understanding of sovereignty – as inadequate, or inefficient, economy – has deep roots in these two earlier plays, where lists and inventories, rather than producing order and stability, contribute to a proliferation of different kinds of *copia* that are never brought into the – to reverse the term – *centripetal* orbit of a unifying sovereign body.

The uses of *copia* start with the first tavern scene in *Henry IV* part one, with Prince Hal taunting Falstaff. It does not let up until the last Act of part two, notably in Falstaff's verbose plans to ingratiate himself with Hal by making fun of Justice Shallow. That very first use of copious rhetoric in the plays – in the tavern scene – immediately gives the troping mechanisms of *copia* a close association with alcohol and drunkenness. Hal responds to Falstaff's question about the time of day:

> Thou art so fat-witted with drinking of old sack, and unbuttoning thee after supper, and sleeping upon benches after noon, that thou hast forgotten to demand that truly which thou wouldst truly know. What a devil hast though to do with the time of day? Unless hours were cups of sack, and minutes capons, and clocks the tongues of bawds, and dials the signs of leaping houses, and the blessed sun himself a fair hot wench in flame-coloured taffeta, I see no reason why thou shouldst be so superfluous to demand the time of day. (1.2.2–10)

'Superfluous' is exactly what Hal is being with his language. Outside of the classic Erasmian version of *copia*, Renaissance rhetorical handbooks are more likely to identify copiousness with superfluity and waste. Richard Sherry lists *pleonasmus* and *perissologia* as vices. He describes the former as 'when ye sentence is laden with superfluous wordes', and the latter as 'when a sentence is added, ye matter thereby never the waightyer'.[8] The dialogue of the two *Henry IV* plays commits both of these rhetorical sins almost constantly. Sherry's assertion that repetition begins to undermine the seriousness of what is being written captures some of what is happening in these two plays. George Puttenham is a little more even-handed in his assessment of *pleonasmus*, which he argues, 'being seasonably used, hath a pretty grace'. However, this is not always the case and, for the most part, he sees it as a significant vice:

> *The vice of surpulsage*; pleonasmus, *or too full speech* . . . the poet or maker's speech becomes vicious and unpleasant by nothing more than by using too much surplusage, and this lieth not only in a word or two more than ordinary but in whole clauses, and peradventure large sentences impertinently spoken, or with more labour and curiosity than is requisite.[9]

Hal's enumeration of examples (not just drinking sack, but also unbuttoning, and sleeping, and forgetting; not just 'hours' as 'cups of sack', but also 'minutes' as 'capons', 'clocks' as 'the tongues of bawds', 'dials' as signposts for brothels, and the 'blessed sun himself' as a prostitute) would be textbook Erasmian *copia* if they did not massively contravene the importance that he places on decorum. What happens with dialogue in the *Henry IV* plays is that the virtues of *copia* are moved in the direction of the vices of *pleonasmus*. In *de Copia*, Erasmus comments that it was Ovid who 'made a feature' of eloquent verbosity, and as a consequence the Roman poet was 'taxed with not knowing when to stop when elaborating an idea'.[10] Erasmus tells us that this tendency to run on beyond what was necessary was what particularly annoyed Seneca about Ovid's style of writing. A similar criticism could quite easily be applied to numerous characters in the *Henry IV* plays, if not to the entirety of the two plays. Hal, Falstaff and – in part one – Hotspur are all especially superfluous in their language, frequently using 'more labour and curiosity than is requisite'. If some of the history plays might be imagined as centripetal in their movement, zooming in on, and putting imaginative pressure on, the individual, isolated figure of a monarch (for example, *Richard II* or *Henry V*), then others might be thought of as centrifugal in their motions. This would be the case with the *Henry IV* plays, where the copious, overinflated language mirrors, and helps to produce, multiple sites of authority, and a narrative that travels rapidly across the length and breadth of England and Wales.

Patricia Parker connects the two plays' interest in dilatory rhetoric, particularly *germination* ('wordy repetition'), with the 'divided body politic' that is depicted in their narratives of rebellion and troubled – inadequate even – succession.[11] Parker also plots her understanding of rhetorical dilation as a form of feminised delay – a digression from successive ends – on to the fat, feminised body of Falstaff: 'Falstaff's fat is repeatedly associated with the copiousness or dilation of discourse, with avoiding the summons of the law through various counterparts of the "dilatory plea," and with the wombs and tongues of women.'[12] It is certainly true that, in the *Henry IV* plays, Falstaff might be considered the cynosure of the plays' many dilations. But he is not the only source of copiousness. The plays' tendencies towards listing, inventory, reckoning, doubling, verbosity and misunderstanding extend beyond Falstaff to cover the whole of King Henry's England. The old knight is, though, a good place to start.

## Falstaff's Drunk Body Politic

Towards the end of the second part of *Henry IV*, Falstaff is in conversation with Prince John, Prince Hal's younger brother. John is fresh from his morally dubious 'victory' over the rebels, in which he has tricked them into dismissing their troops on the false promise of a peace treaty. He persuades the Archbishop of York, and other rebels against Henry IV, that 'My father's purposes have been mistook', and that 'some about him have too lavishly / Wrested his meaning and authority' (4.1.221–3). The rebels understand this to mean that Prince John is willing to negotiate with them, and to accommodate their demands. This apparent understanding convinces them that they should dismiss the armies that they had gathered to oppose the king. John takes advantage of this, quibbles with the promises he has just made – which we have also heard him make – and arrests all of the rebels for treason. We would, these days, say that he is 'gaslighting' them. As one of the rebels, Mowbray, asks, echoing the reaction of an audience that might have expected something a bit more honourable: 'Is this just and reasonable?' (4.1.275). G. Wilson Knight describes John's strategic sleight of hand as 'a dastardly act of treachery'.[13] In the next scene, John continues to act on behalf of the king. He is returning to London, and encounters a typically belated Falstaff on the way, warning him that 'These tardy tricks of yours will, on my life, / One time or other break some gallows' back' (4.2.23–4). Falstaff, for his part, claims that he has done his part by capturing an enemy prisoner, Coleville. The audience has, however, seen Coleville give himself up willingly to Falstaff earlier in the scene, and John rightly tells Falstaff that 'It was more of his courtesy than your deserving' (4.2.43). But despite this admission of Coleville's 'courtesy', and even though Coleville tells John that he was, essentially, 'just following orders' when he took up arms, the young prince sends Falstaff's prisoner to be executed:

> Send Coleville with his confederates
> To York, to present execution.
> Blunt lead him hence and see you guard him sure.
> And now dispatch we toward the court, my lords:
> I hear the King my father is sore sick. (4.2.71–5)

There might have been some military rationale for John's behaviour in the earlier scene. Paul Jorgensen shows how Shakespeare's largely uncritical, if not exactly celebratory, depiction of apparently underhanded military strategy would have echoed developments in Elizabethan warfare in the 1590s, particularly with regard to English campaigns in Ireland.[14] But this next scene, the exchange with Falstaff, makes it clear that there is more at stake than the expedient strategising of a military leader. In the scene in which John encounters Falstaff, he twice threatens capital punishment: once to Falstaff, and secondly to Falstaff's prisoner, Coleville. The scene is, in fact, suffused with the threats of judicial violence upon which sovereign authority depends. Prince John, however, is, at the very least, compromised as a locus of sovereignty. He acts on behalf of his father, but in a manner that goes behind the backs of his own side as well as tricking their opponents. John's compromised authority is one aspect of the degenerated sovereignty that characterises both *Henry IV* plays.

It is into this scene, already freighted with an atmosphere that fosters a dark cynicism about the workings of sovereign authority, that Falstaff launches his most joyously sceptical speech of the two plays, surpassing his critique of 'honour' in the first play with an invective that is this time aimed, not just at the hypocrisies of assuming chivalric values, but at the heart of the body politic itself. Left to soliloquise, he takes both stage and opportunity. The problem with Prince John, he tells us, is that he doesn't drink enough:

> There's never none of these demure boys come to any proof; for thin drink doth so overcool their blood, and making many fish meals, that they fall into a kind of male green-sickness; and then when they marry, they get wenches. They are generally fools and cowards—which some of us should be too, but for inflammation. (4.2.75–9)

John is effeminate, enervated and anaemic because he doesn't drink sack, Falstaff's version of a universal panacea. His own apparent lack of cowardice he puts down to the 'inflammation' caused by excess drinking. In the comic misreading of humoral theory that runs throughout the soliloquy, Falstaff understands the overheating effects of alcohol as a form of restorative that allows both him and the country to function properly. Picking 'sherry-sack' as his drink of choice, he lists its properties: first that it makes you witty and second that it prevents cowardice. He then extends his description of sack's positive effects on the body into a lengthy, but tipsy, 'body politic' metaphor:

> But the sherry warms it, and makes it course from the inwards to the parts' extremes; it illuminateth the face, which, as a beacon, gives warning to all the rest of this little kingdom, man, to arm; and then the vital commoners and inland petty spirits muster me all to their captain, the heart; who, great

and puffed up with his retinue, doth any deed of courage. And this valour comes of sherry. So that skill in the weapon is nothing without sack, for that sets it a-work; and learning a mere hoard of gold kept by a devil, till sack commences it and sets it in act and use. Hereof comes it that Prince Harry is valiant; for the cold blood he did naturally inherit of his father he hath like lean, sterile, and bare land, manured, husbanded, and tilled, with excellent endeavour of drinking good, and good store of fertile sherry, that he is become very hot and valiant. (4.2.87–99)

The elaboration of this metaphor in which the effects of alcohol are imagined as the oil in the machine of a sovereign – and centralising – monarchical state is ironic in its immediate context: Falstaff absurdly claiming courage and a concern for the nation. But it is also much more broadly ironic within the context of the play as a whole.

Falstaff's soliloquy comes at the moment when Prince John is in the process of returning to the dying centre of the English monarchy: his father's deathbed. As I have intimated, even if Falstaff's criticisms of the prince are themselves inaccurate and lacking in moral authority, John is hardly a figure who is exempt from the attacks. If it is clear, from his actions, that he is not a 'fool', it is far from clear that he is not a 'coward'. Throughout these two scenes, John is engaged in the archetypal act of sovereign justice – ordering executions – but he is also shown to be acting on dubious grounds, if not legally, then morally. In this marginal meeting between Falstaff and John, somewhere on the road between the royal court and the battlefield, the securing of sovereign decision making to a coherent and unified body politic is rendered specious. This is sovereignty on the fly, improvised and lacking in security.

Both *Henry IV* plays, but part two in particular, feature continual and restless movements away from the centre, taking in the borderlands of Wales, the suburbs of London, the tavern at Eastcheap, the rebel courts and battlefields of Northumberland, Shrewsbury, Yorkshire and Gloucestershire, as well as the royal court. They cover more ground than any of the other history plays, and these centrifugal movements of the plot find a representational equivalent in the play's vagrant bodies and hyper-extended forms of *copia*. E. M. W. Tillyard describes Falstaff's 'disquisition on sherris-sack' as 'a perfectly correct parody of the physical organisation of the microcosm and of its correspondence with another sphere of existence, the body politic'.[15] And it is true that Falstaff's mock body politic is centralising in its impetus, imagining the heart as 'captain' of his drunken kingdom. But to delimit this speech simply as a parody of a discourse that might be perfectly operable elsewhere in the play is to miss the extent to which the play resists the stability of microcosm and analogy, preferring instead a freewheeling movement away from what is a constantly collapsing centre.

Rebecca Lemon reads Falstaff's drunk body-politic speech as an encomium to alcohol, written within a tradition of defences of drinking as something that produces convivial sociability. But she also records the problems that are associated with such defences both here and elsewhere in early modern England. As convivial drinking tips over into habit, 'Formerly self-sovereign, the habitual drinker becomes overtaken, enslaved, and addicted.'[16] Lemon follows Falstaff's downfall through addiction to sack as a narrative that belongs to Falstaff alone, arguing that Shakespeare 'stages, in the rejection of Falstaff, a moral position he does not necessarily embrace'.[17] Falstaff does become progressively more sack-obsessed throughout the two plays, and he does seem to become a more morally dubious character. However, the rest of the play's action is not at all free from the implications of misgovernment that accompany Falstaff's sack addiction.

Benjamin Bertram considers the broader implications of Falstaff's drunken body politic, placing it within the traditions of a convivial sociability, 'the shared experience of pleasure in the act of drinking, eating, and conversing', that might work against the hierarchical structures of the Lancastrian monarchy.[18] Bertram argues, however, that Falstaff is unsuccessful in the plays because his particular language of excessive consumption cannot accommodate itself to the way that Hal ultimately brings together the hierarchies of the traditional monarchical body politic with those of the new 'little kingdom' through which the new world of trade was to work from the late sixteenth century onwards. Even if Falstaff's drunken body politic might involve imagining, as Bertram writes, 'new possibilities for social bonds that are not based on the fixed hierarchies of an organic community', it is Hal who emerges with the authority to control the coming world.[19] Like me, Bertram sees this in terms of centripetal and centrifugal forces; he writes of Falstaff's drunken body politic speech that 'If the description of Falstaff works as a centrifugal force, that of the traditional body politic performs the opposite function.'[20]

But in looking at the way that *copia* – 'surplusage' even – metastasises through the language of these two plays, it is not so clear that the monarchy, that sovereign power itself, is rescued from the hangover of Falstaff's words. Even if Falstaff is, himself, drunk, the speech is correct in its inference that the whole body politic is also 'drunk'. Political language in these plays wheels out of control. Images of sickness and bodily dysfunction proliferate throughout both Henry IV's kingdom and the play's dialogue. While Falstaff might epitomise this more general sense of disorder, he exemplifies, rather than transcends, the world of these plays.

## Vagrant Bodies in Henry IV's England

Links between a disorderly kingdom and fragile human bodies begin with the opening four lines of *Henry IV* part one:

> KING So shaken as we are, so wan with care,
> Find we a time for frighted peace to pant
> And breathe short-winded accents of new broils
> To be commenced in strands afar remote. (1.1.1–4)

At first, it sounds as though the king is describing only himself as 'shaken', but Henry's royal 'we' is extended to include a sense of the whole nation as exhausted, but still expecting the foreign wars that are now being planned. The king's personal frailty remains as an emblem of the kingdom's fragility from this moment in the very opening lines of the play right through to Act 5. The rebels have sent Westmorland as a messenger before the battle of Shrewsbury, and Henry receives him reluctantly:

> KING You have deceived our trust,
> And made us doff our easy robes of peace
> To crush our old limbs in ungentle steel.
> This is not well, my lord, this is not well.
> What say you to it? (5.1.11–16)

Again, the focus on Henry's failing health, something that becomes an even more prominent aspect of *Henry IV* part two, doubles as an image of the ailing and failing nation, forced against its will to take up arms. The fragmentary pronouns that were a feature of Richard's dialogue in *Richard II* marked, in that play and for that king, a movement of inward collapse, a self-defeating image of only apparently self-consistent sovereignty. Here, the 'we' seems to envelop the country in a more comprehensive way, assuming a consonance between king and kingdom. But what Henry does is to assume that the country is as sick as he is.

The connection between a sickening kingdom and the dying king is made still more explicit in *Henry IV* part two. In the sequel, Warwick claims that the country, at least, can be cured of its 'rank diseases' by 'cooling' some of its rebels:

> KING HENRY Then you perceive the body of our kingdom,
> How foul it is, what rank diseases grow,

And with what danger near the heart of it.
WARWICK It is but as a body yet distempered,
Which to his former strength may be restored
With good advice and little medicine.
My Lord Northumberland will soon be cooled. (3.1.37–43)

Warwick describes a body that is 'distempered', its humoral balance wrong, or with an imbalance in its component parts. The king receives Warwick's projected 'restoration' sceptically, however, and the later, central and emblematic scene of part two – the scene in the king's sickroom – provides a dramatic focus for the atmosphere of deterioration, exhaustion and sickness that pervades both plays. As Henry is revealed in his sickbed, his opening speech continues to conflate and confuse his own failing body with that of the kingdom:

KING HENRY Now, lords, if God doth give successful end
To this debate that bleedeth at our doors,
We will our youth lead on to higher fields,
And draw no swords but what are sanctified.
Our navy is addressed, our power collected,
Our substitutes in absence well invested,
And everything lies level to our wish;
Only we want a little personal strength,
And pause us till these rebels now afoot
Come underneath the yoke of government. (4.3.1–10)

Henry is restating what are, by this point, his rather tired and unrealistic plans for a crusade to the Holy Land. The rebellion that has caused the kingdom to 'pause' a little in these plans has, of course, taken up the whole of two plays and the whole of Henry's reign. The proposed crusade was announced as penance for the act of deposing Richard II that initiated his reign, and he is still harping on it on his deathbed. Implied in this speech is a 'body politic' analogy, with Henry using the royal 'we' flexibly to incorporate his own sick body and the workings of sovereignty throughout the kingdom. But disjunctions appear from the very start – between, for example, the apparently personal 'our doors' and the phrase 'our youth' in the next line. The pronoun used for the private spaces of the royal sickbed is suddenly opened out to include the potential, and largely imaginary, armies of youth that he will have at his disposal once the rebels are brought under control. And 'youth' sounds oddly here, from the mouth of a dying and compromised king. The compromised nature of his position, something that has followed him throughout his reign and the two plays, is indicated in the caveat that, only from now on, will his swords be 'sanctified'.

When he begins to consider the need to install deputies to operate on his behalf, the body politic analogy comes under further pressure. If, in his 'absence', those deputised to act on his behalf are 'well invested', then the lack of 'a little personal strength' might not matter. But throughout this speech and elsewhere in the two plays, Henry's use of the royal 'we' fails fully to secure a consistent relationship between his own person and the kingdom. Here, as he speaks from the most private space represented in any of Shakespeare's history plays – the bed of the king – the bleeding kingdom lies beyond 'our doors'. Henry's admission that he lacks 'a little personal strength' does not merely give the lie to his confident claim that 'everything lies level to our wish', it also opens up a space for considering the relative claims of the different uses of 'our' throughout the speech. To what extent are the following things that belong properly to Henry, as sovereign, or things that are now beyond the doors of his sickbed, and beyond his control: 'our doors', 'our youth', 'our navy', 'our substitutes', 'our wish', '[our] personal strength'? If the rebels are to come under the 'yoke of government', whose government will it be?

## Centrifugal Movement in the *Henry IV* Plays

King Henry's deathbed is the scene that represents, in the most concentrated form, the sense of enervation that pervades the two plays. This impression of a failing centre, however, is also provided by the restless movement of the plays' action. The alternating movements in part one – between court, tavern and the Welsh border country – realise some of this. But the sense of agitated movement is vastly intensified in part two where locations move from court to tavern, city to country, from border areas to roadways. The unusual opening chorus from the figure of Rumour announces this in the opening words of the play:

> Open your ears; for which of you will stop
> The vent of hearing when loud Rumour speaks?
> I from the orient to the drooping west,
> Making the wind my post-horse, still unfold
> The acts commenced on this ball of earth. (1.1–5)[21]

The primary message of this opening is, of course, that news (and history) can be rendered inaccurate by the particular means of communication employed. The speech plunges into a world of rapidly developing events, and also produces an idea of irascible movement. The figure of Rumour imagines itself to be a kind of angry Robin Goodfellow, a mischievous principle of warlike vagrancy, bringing the supposed final victory at Shrewsbury, the conclusion to part one, into a world of extreme agitation:

> I run before King Henry's victory,
> Who in a bloody field by Shrewsbury
> That beaten down young Hotspur and his troops,
> Quenching the flame of bold rebellion
> Even with the rebels' blood. But what mean I
> To speak so true at first? My office is
> To noise abroad that Harry Monmouth's fell
> Under the wrath of noble Hotspur's sword,
> And that the King before the Douglas' rage
> Stooped his anointed head as low as death.
> This have I rumoured through the peasant towns
> Between that royal field of Shrewsbury
> And this worm-eaten hole of ragged stone
> Where Hotspur's father, old Northumberland,
> Lies crafty-sick. The posts come tiring on,
> And not a man of them brings other news
> Than they have learnt of me. (1.23–39)

Rumour's 'office' might be to spread false information about the results of civil war, thus increasing the factionalism of the warring parties. But the effect of the scene is to generate, for the audience, the rapid movements that are also entailed in the play's frequent shifts of scene. The first scene, following Rumour's chorus, confirms the atmosphere of insecurity and decentredness that has already been introduced. The play opens, not in the royal court, but at the home of one of the rebels – the 'worm-eaten hole of ragged stone' where Northumberland, Hotspur's father, is, according to Rumour, malingering.

The first messenger to arrive from Shrewsbury is Lord Bardolph who delivers the false news of the rebels' victory. He is immediately contradicted by the next arrival at Northumberland's castle, Travers, who rightly informs the earl of the rebels' loss and the death of Harry Percy (Hotspur), Northumberland's son. Travers, however, spends most of his speech charting his own movements and the pathways that information has taken:

> TRAVERS My lord, Sir John Umfrevile turned me back
> With joyful tidings, and being better horsed
> Outrode me. After him came spurring hard
> A gentleman almost forspent with speed,
> That stopped by me to breath his bloodied horse.
> He asked the way to Chester, and of him
> I did demand what news from Shrewsbury.
> He told me that rebellion had bad luck,
> And that young Harry Percy's spur was cold.

With that he gave his able horse the head,
And, bending forward, struck his armed heels
Against the panting sides of his poor jade
Up to the rowel-head; and starting so,
He seemed in running to devour the way,
Staying no longer question. (1.1.34–48)

Although the correct information about the battle with which part one closed is finally given, this is a piece of narrative exposition that is heavily mediated and might leave even well-informed audience members a little unsure of what has happened prior to the action of this play. The main impression left by Travers's speech is one of confused, restless and rapid motion, with participants in the action of the civil war criss-crossing the country in ever more confused ways. Each of the encounters that Travers describes is marked by a kind of excess – turning back, outriding, 'forspent with speed', 'running to devour the way'. This is a play that, more than any other of the history plays, takes place on the road and on the hoof. As Northumberland says on first greeting Lord Bardolph, 'The times are wild; contention, like a horse / Full of high feeding, madly hath broke loose / And bears down all before him' (1.1.9–11). 'Contention' – civil war – has set the whole country on the move. This unmooring of clear lines of communication is a narrative correlative for the centrifugal force of the plays' peripatetic uses of *copia* and conforms with the later illustrations of misaligned forms of deputation and sovereignty seen, for example, in the scene between Prince John and Falstaff already described. That scene, like Travers's exhausting encounters on horseback, is set somewhere out on the road.

## Henry IV Part Two: 'as a dog returneth to his vomit'

Shakespeare's use of *copia* in the two *Henry IV* plays is excessive, then, in a manner that undermines the security of any singular image of sovereignty. There are also ways in which forms of excess are an aspect of Shakespeare's writing practices between the three different printed texts of *Henry IV* part two. The textual history of the second part of *Henry IV* is particularly rich, given the existence of these three texts: a first quarto printed in 1600 that omits the scene usually numbered as Act 3, scene 1 in modern editions; a second quarto that was printed very quickly in the same year, but which includes that scene; and the folio text that, in addition to that scene, also has several lengthy passages that are not in either quarto. The story that the three different editions seems to tell is one in which an original text has been somewhat censored, but also one in which Shakespeare is always extending his material, with the missing scene from the first quarto potentially being a late addition from Shakespeare, and some of the additional passages in the folio being inserted between an initial version of the play and the version that found its way into the folio. Jowett and Taylor identify the folio text of the play as 'the culmination of a process of conscious revision initiated even before a fair copy was begun'.[22] The process is not dissimilar to that which seems to have been undertaken with *Henry VI* part two, as detailed in the Introduction.

One of the most remarkable of the extra passages in *Henry IV* part two comes right at the end of the first scene of the opening Act, a scene in which the rebels against the king are weighing up their chances of success in any potential fight. If it did predate the quartos, then it may have been cut from the 1600 quarto texts because of its political sensitivity. The scene also introduces ideas of sickness, infirmity and old age in the person of the Earl of Northumberland. Northumberland is walking on crutches and wearing a nightcap; he receives conflicting accounts of his son Hotspur's death. His promise, at the end of the scene, to commit further to the cause of the rebellion and to take up arms echoes the king's lines from the end of the previous play, in which he has claimed that the rebels have 'made us doff our easy robes of peace / To crush our old limbs in ungentle steel'. Here, the Earl of Northumberland, on finally realising that his son is indeed dead, puts down the props and signs of old age and infirmity, replacing them with armour:

NORTHUMBERLAND For this I shall have time enough to mourn.
In poison there is physic; and these news,
Having been well, that would have made me sick,
Being sick, have in some measure made me well;
And, as the wretch whose fever-weakened joints,
Like strengthless hinges, buckle under life,
Impatient of his fit, breaks like a fire
Out of his keeper's arms, even so my limbs,
Weakened with grief, being now enraged with grief,
Are thrice themselves.
     *[He casts away his crutch]*
       Hence therefore, thou nice crutch!
A scaly gauntlet now with joints of steel
Must glove this hand.
     *[He removes his coif]*
       And hence, thou sickly coif!
Thou art a guard too wanton for the head
Which princes fleshed with conquest aim to hit.
Now bind my brows with iron, and approach

The ragged'st hour that time and spite dare bring
To frown upon th'enraged Northumberland! (1.1.136–52)

As Northumberland gives an account of his own physical and emotional transformation, he also gives, in an extended form of metonymy, a very attenuated version of the body-politic metaphor. His body, and the body of the rebellious kingdom, are imagined as a convulsive invalid, 'buckling' under the restrictions of sickness to achieve a strength that is almost empty, or that is something more like the uncanny strength of an automaton. The extreme contrasting images of sickliness and strength – 'strengthless hinges' being clothed in 'joints of steel'; a 'sickly coif' (nightcap) being exchanged for bands of iron – are more than just a picture of Northumberland's grief, frustration and determination as he plans to make a final stand against the Lancastrian regime. The extended metaphor of the patient on his sickbed, breaking free of his keeper's control, whose limbs are both 'strengthless' and, uncannily, 'thrice themselves', is also an image of failing sovereignty. It prefigures the final scenes of Henry himself, appearing on stage in bed, unable to come good on his continuing promises to lead a crusade. Northumberland's language plays with multiple ideas of mastery and servitude, both in terms of the submission that the country has had to make to whom he sees as the Lancastrian imposter, but also in terms of how his body is controlled. His fellow rebels are concerned: 'This strainèd passion doth you wrong', Umfreville tells him, in a line that is only in the quarto texts of the play.[23] Lord Bardolph and Morton both see Northumberland's spasmodic attempts to muster his strength as more problematic than sustaining for the rebels' cause:

LORD BARDOLPH Sweet Earl, divorce not wisdom from your honour.
MORTON The lives of all your loving complices
Lean on your health, the which, if you give o'er
To stormy passion, must perforce decay. (1.1.161–6)

Preaching the wisdom of Aristotelian moderation, Lord Bardolph and Morton consider Northumberland's grief-motivated strength to be something that will only lead to further decay, rather than act as a means to reinvigorate the rebellion.

Into this scene which, from the beginning of *Henry IV* part two, has ensured that the play is a much darker affair than many of the other history plays, Shakespeare and Morton launch one of the most troubling speeches of the whole sequence of history plays. This is a speech that is only available in the folio, likely to have been suppressed from the two quarto texts because of its treatment of rebellion:

> The gentle Archbishop of York is up
> With well-appointed powers. He is a man
> Who with a double surety binds his followers.
> My lord, your son had only but the corpse,
> But shadows and the shows of men, to fight;
> For that same word 'rebellion' did divide
> The action of their bodies from their souls,
> And they did fight with queasiness, constrained,
> As men drink potions, that their weapons only
> Seemed on our side; but, for their spirits and souls,
> This word 'rebellion', it had froze them up,
> As fish are in a pond. But now the Bishop
> Turns insurrection to religion.
> Supposed sincere and holy in his thoughts,
> He's followed both with body and with mind,
> And doth enlarge his rising with the blood of Pomfret stones;
> Derives from heaven his quarrel and his cause;
> Tells them he doth bestride a bleeding land
> Gasping for life under great Bolingbroke;
> And more and less do flock to follow him. (1.1.A1–A21)[24]

Attempting to persuade Northumberland of the likely success of any future rebellion, Morton imagines something that is not available anywhere else in the political language of these two plays – a unity between body and soul, between intent and action. Where, formerly, the soldiers on the side of the rebels had 'the action of their bodies' divided from 'their souls', it has taken the strong religious persuasions of the Archbishop of York to draw a kind of double unity together, a unity between intention and action, and also between different levels of society: 'more and less do flock to follow him'. The sacramental image of Richard's blood has, in the words and actions of the archbishop, become a catalyst for an embodied sovereignty in which actions are finally consonant with will. Henry himself is never able, throughout the play, to draw on this kind of confident language, his speech instead being all about mismatches between action and intention, failing bodies and ill-fitting armour.

Just two scenes later, however, Morton's apparent confidence in the archbishop's offers of unification are given the lie. In a speech that is again only available in the folio text, and not in the two quarto texts from 1600, the Archbishop of York bitterly criticises the capriciousness of the English people – the 'fond many' – who seem too often to shift allegiances. He despises their capacity to switch from Richard II to Henry IV, only now, after Richard's deposition and murder, to mourn the loss of their former king. He makes this criticism even as he suggests that the rebels exploit the people's newfound disenchantment with their new king in order to explain and promote their own opposition to

Henry IV. The strategic point, however, is lost underneath a network of images and metaphors that link the fate of kings to eating and sickness:

> ARCHBISHOP                          Let us on,
> And publish the occasion of our arms.
> The commonwealth is sick of their own choice;
> Their over-greedy love hath surfeited.
> An habitation giddy and unsure
> Hath he that buildeth on the vulgar heart.
> O thou fond many, with what loud applause
> Didst thou beat heaven with blessing Bolingbroke,
> Before he was what thou wouldst have him be?
> And being now trimmed in thine own desires,
> Thou, beastly feeder, art so full of him
> That thou provok'st thyself to cast him up.
> So, so, thou common dog, didst thou disgorge
> Thy glutton bosom of the royal Richard,
> And now thou wouldst eat thy dead vomit up,
> And howl'st to find it. What trust is in these times?
> They that, when Richard lived, would have him die
> Are now become enamoured on his grave.
> Thou that threw'st dust upon his goodly head
> When through proud London he came sighing on
> After th'admired heels of Bolingbroke,
> Cry'st now, 'O earth, yield us that King again
> And take thou this!' O thoughts of men accursed!
> Past and to come seems best; things present, worst. (1.3.85–108)[25]

The striking image of the 'commons' as a 'beastly feeder' that forces itself to be sick after gorging on Bolingbroke and that now, dog-like, returns to eat its own vomit, is biblical in origin. The famous verse from Proverbs is 'As a dogge turneth againe to his owne vomite, so a foole turneth to his foolishness' (Prov. 26.11). The archbishop is, then, accusing the English people not only of a beastly feeding, but also of mass stupidity, not understanding what it is doing with these fickle changes of heart. The biblical proverb resolves the image of the dog eating its own vomit into an emblematic image of foolishness. That is, the stupidity of the dog is more important to its sense than the idea, on its own, of a dog eating its own vomit. However, typically for Shakespeare, he extends the metaphor at the expense of its literal sense, giving more life to the idea of a body that eats, vomits and eats again than to the tenor of the metaphor; the vehicle of the metaphor eclipses the idea of the populace's stupidity in the archbishop's speech. The speech is overburdened with images of excess, of excessive eating, and of regurgitation. Even as the archbishop's disdain for the stupidity of the English people is made obvious, the lingering impression of his speech is that the succession of

English kings can be understood as a form of alimentary breakdown, a digestive disorder. Each word seems to curve into the gravitational pull of the metaphor's semantic field, so that when Bolingbroke is said now to be 'trimmed' to the desires of the people, the word suggests not merely that he has been prepared to serve their wishes, but that he has been prepared for being eaten at the dinner table.

That both Shakespeare and the archbishop are considering succession more broadly than the particular issues of rebellion, usurpation, and the inconstancy of crowds that are to hand can be seen in the images of perverse resurrection at the end of the speech. The people cry out for the earth to give Richard back to them, his own Christ-like delusions being perversely realised in the conjunction of the commonwealth's desire for constant change and the grievances of the Yorkist rebels. In *Richard II*, Richard had pointlessly implored the earth to come to his aid as he arrived back on the shores of Wales from Ireland. The archbishop now sees the crowd's love for the usurped king as similarly hopeless. But as he contemplates rebelling against a current ruler to restore the order of a former line of succession, it is at best an eccentric position for him to take, to criticise the popular sentiment, 'Past and to come seems best; things present, worst' as 'accursed'. As a leading rebel, he is eager to restore the Yorkist line to the throne, to bring about a future based on the past and to eradicate the Lancastrian 'things present'. 'Past and to come' are always, for rebels, better than things present, and the sentiments that he sees as foolish are precisely his own. The archbishop, as much as the English people, is like a dog returning to his own vomit.

John Jowett and Gary Taylor argue that this particular speech, only available in the folio and not in the two 1600 quartos of the play, was not, as some speeches were, omitted through censorship but was a Shakespearean addition to the script some time between 1600 and 1623. In a manner similar to *Henry VI* part two, Shakespeare expands and extrapolates the original material. With the later play, he seems particular keen to, as Jowett and Taylor write, look backward, 'emphasising the links with his own earlier history plays'.[26] There is a sense in which the plays, themselves, see Shakespeare returning like a dog to his own vomit. The patterns of recursion and repetition mimic the dysfunctional succession that the archbishop outlines in his speech: dysfunctional but unavoidable.

In the next chapter, I examine the play with the most troubling and, for Elizabethans, the most consequential set of successions to the crown: *Richard III*. This is a play that, more than any other of the history plays, places a single figure – Richard himself – to the forefront of our attention. And yet his rule is entirely illegitimate, the body that supports his claims to a self-sufficient sovereignty is imagined through copious animal comparisons, and his actions are surrounded by a chorus of multiple female figures. More, perhaps, even than *Richard II*, this play places the supposed ipseity of decisionist sovereignty under scrutiny.

## Notes

1. Nicholas Crawford, 'The Discourse of Dilution in *2 Henry IV*', *Renaissance Papers* (2002), p. 61.
2. Crawford, 'The Discourse of Dilution', p. 68.
3. Robert Grudin, 'Liberty of Ideas: Renaissance Copia and the Nature of Free Thought', *Writing on the Edge* 5.1 (1993), p. 34.
4. Grudin, 'Liberty of Ideas', p. 35.
5. Grudin, 'Liberty of Ideas', p. 36.
6. Terence Cave, *The Cornucopian Text: Problems of Writing in the French Renaissance* (Oxford: Oxford University Press, 1985), p. 34.
7. Jeffrey J. Yu, 'Shakespeare's *Julius Caesar*, Erasmus's *Copia*, and Sentential Ambiguity', *Comparative Drama* 41.1 (2007), p. 104.
8. Richard Sherry, *A Treatise of Schemes and Tropes* (London, 1550), sig. B4r.
9. George Puttenham, 'The Art of English Poesy', in *Sidney's The Defence of Poesy and Selected Renaissance Literary Criticism*, ed. Gavin Alexander (Harmondsworth: Penguin, 2004), p. 192.
10. Desidirius Erasmus, *Literary and Educational Writings Volume 2: de Copia*, ed. Craig R. Thompson (Toronto: University of Toronto Press, 2016), p. 299.
11. Patricia Parker, *Literary Fat Ladies: Rhetoric, Gender, Property* (London: Methuen, 1987), p. 72.
12. Parker, *Literary Fat Ladies*, p. 21.
13. G. Wilson Knight, *The Olive and the Sword: A Study of England's Shakespeare* (Oxford: Oxford University Press, 1944), p. 27.
14. Paul A. Jorgensen, 'The "Dastardly Treachery" of Prince John of Lancaster', *PMLA* 76.5 (1961), pp. 488–92.
15. E. M. W. Tillyard, *Shakespeare's History Plays* (London: Chatto and Windus, 1959), p. 288.
16. Rebecca Lemon, 'Sacking Falstaff', in David B. Goldstein and Amy L. Tigner (eds), *Culinary Shakespeare: Staging Food and Drink in Early Modern England* (Pittsburgh: Duquesne University Press, 2016), p. 126.
17. Lemon, 'Sacking Falstaff', p. 130.
18. Bertram, 'Falstaff's Body', p. 299.
19. Bertram, 'Falstaff's Body', p. 305.
20. Bertram, 'Falstaff's Body', p. 301.
21. Elsewhere, for ease of comparison with other editions, I am using Act and scene numbers when citing the *New Oxford Shakespeare* edition of *Henry VI* part two. For this opening Chorus, it seems more sensible to adopt the *New Oxford* editors' preferred method of only designating scene numbers, not Act numbers, for this play.

22. John Jowett and Gary Taylor, 'The Three Texts of *2 Henry VI*', *Studies in Bibliography* 40 (1987), p. 50.
23. This character was revised out of the folio texts and does not appear anywhere else in the quartos. It is assumed that his role was, at some point, subsumed within that of Lord Bardolph.
24. The *Oxford New Shakespeare* editors include this folio-only speech even though they are using the second quarto as their copy text because of their contention that it is the product of earlier censorship rather than of later Shakespearean elaboration. The 'A' designation is for 'Addition'.
25. William Shakespeare, *King Henry IV Part Two*, ed. James C. Bulman (London: Bloomsbury, 2016). I have taken this quotation from the third Arden edition. Elsewhere, I have used the *New Oxford* edition. However, the editors of that edition take the quarto text as their copy text and have only included speeches exclusive to the folio if they believe them to have been previously censored from the quarto texts. This is not something that they believe to be the case with this speech. The Oxford edition will include the folio text of the play when it publishes its volume of 'Alternative Texts'; this is not yet available.
26. Jowett and Taylor, 'The Three Texts of *2 Henry IV*', p. 49.

# Chapter 5

# 'My kingdom for a horse': Bestial Sovereignty in *Richard III*

> ... vacuous
> Ceremony of possession, restless
> Habitation, no man's resting place.
>
> Geoffrey Hill, 'Funeral Music'[1]

Richard's final words in *Richard III* are among Shakespeare's most famous lines. 'A horse, a horse, my kingdom for a horse!' (5.6.7) Richard shouts, as he enters what is the very brief penultimate scene of the play, repeating his appeal as he exits just six lines later. He then re-enters in the next scene for the sword fight in which Richmond, the future Henry VII, kills him. 'The days is ours; the bloody dog is dead', the Tudor victor declares (5.7.2). Richard does not say anything in this scene. His willingness to give up everything that he has gained for the chance of an escape on horseback appears, to us, an expression of utter desperation. But it would probably have had darkly, but distinctly, comic implications for its first audiences. The fate of Richard's body immediately after the events depicted at the end of Shakespeare's play were well known. The king's naked body was tied to the back of a horse that was then driven from the battlefield to the town of Leicester. Polydore Vergil, the historian hired by Henry VII, writes that

> the body of king Rycherd nakyd of all clothing, and layd upon an horse bake with the armes and legges hanging downe on both sydes, was browght to thabbay of monks Franciscanes at Leycester, a myserable spectacle in good sooth, but not unworthy for the mans lyfe, and ther was buryed two days after without any pompe or solemne funerall.[2]

In death and in disgrace, Richard's body has become first a piece of luggage, transported on the back of a horse, and then an ignominious spectacle. Thomas More's history of Richard III adds that the defeated Yorkist was 'harried on horseback dead, his hair in despite torn and tugged like a cur dog'.[3] At the end of Shakespeare's play, Richmond takes his cue from More when he refers to Richard as a 'bloody dog'. Richmond is the spokesperson for the Tudor triumphalism that the real Henry VII inaugurated, that More builds into the received historiography of Richard III, and that Shakespeare was also following: a country rescued from a beastly dog of a tyrant by a noble leader.

Philip Schwyzer, writing about the ways in which the remains of Richard III have been construed through history, makes the point that 'The exhibition of the dead king's torn and naked body had an impact on collective memory, well beyond those who might actually have witnessed the spectacle.'[4] Schwyzer insists that 'For most English people before Shakespeare's play, mention of the body of Richard III would bring to mind not the image of a halting hunchback, but that of a naked corpse on a horse's rump.'[5] The naked Richard, transported on horseback as a piece of luggage, is the antithesis of the king-as-horseman, powerful symbol of sovereign control, an image obliquely presented earlier in the play when Buckingham warns against a state in which horses are allowed to govern themselves:

> Where every horse bears his commanding rein
> And may direct his course as please himself,
> As well the fear of harm as harm apparent,
> In my opinion, ought to be prevented. (2.2.128–31)

Here, Buckingham is disingenuously warning against the young Prince Edward being paraded in front of the people on his way to the Tower. But, however self-serving Buckingham is being here, the image of a horse that is in control of its rider comes readily to hand as an image of usurped sovereignty, of a world turned upside down. At Richard's demise, his 'commanding rein' is truly given over to being borne by the horse, rather than the other way around. Those in Shakespeare's audience who did recollect the ignominious end of the charismatic king might then very well have had a bitter and sardonic laugh at Richard's desperate pleas for a horse as he stumbles around the field at Bosworth. He would be getting that ride on a horse soon enough, they might have thought.

Shakespeare does not stage Richard's final humiliation. And, as the conflicting opinions of editors would seem to suggest, it is not entirely clear from printed versions of the text what happens to Richard's body on stage. The editors of the *New Oxford Shakespeare* write of the stage direction 'Richard is slain' that lies between the two scenes that '[Richmond] might leave Richard's body on stage, to be addressed as "this bloody wretch" at 5.7.5, but it may instead be removed' (5.6.14. sd.n.). Successive Arden editions have included the stage direction that 'Richard's body is removed', but there is no real need for this to be included, despite the contention that the final scene has to take place in a different location to the 'kingdom for a horse' scene. The note on the third Arden edition, citing the precedent of Alexander Dyce, reads as follows:

> Since Richmond re-enters with Stanley who bears Richard's crown from the site of his death, they enter to a different fictional location than that of the killing (Dyce); Richard's corpse would therefore have been removed. The phrase this bloody wretch (5) does not demand presence.[6]

It seems to me, however, that neither the practical demands of staging the final scenes, nor any particular need to maintain the fictional integrity of the play's locations, which are everywhere rather generalised, absolutely demand one solution over the other. It may be that his corpse is left on stage as Henry Tudor triumphs in the closing scene of the play, underscoring the claim that the new king and his bride, Elizabeth, are the 'true succeeders of each royal house', and are repairing the damage done by 'divided York and Lancaster' (5.5.30, 27), with a reminder of what happens to false usurpers who seek to exploit, rather than repair, the divisions of civil strife.

This would make a neat counter-scene to Richard's wooing of Anne over the hearse of Henry VI early in the play. In both scenes, the dead bodies of kings furnish the scenery for the emergence of a new order. Or it might be that his body is cleared off stage, giving Richmond free rein to speak directly to the audience about the glories of a Tudor-led England. However, as Richmond asks after the 'men of name' who have been 'slain on either side', and gives orders to 'Inter their bodies as become their births', then either the presence or the memory of Richard's abject body might provide a potentially ironic note (5.7.12, 15). Richard is not to be treated in a manner that is consonant with his birth; his body will not be interred as becomes his birth. Rather, it is shoved off to one side, collateral damage in the journey towards Tudor victory.

Greta Olson writes that 'Like hardly another character in Shakespearean drama, Richard III commands the audience's attention to his body.'[7] This has, indeed, been the case, with his limping gait and physical centrality to most scenes providing for a compelling performance. Vergil's officially sanctioned history lingers over Richard's physicality at the end of the account of his reign:

> He was lyttle of stature, deformyd of body, thone showlder being higher than thother, a short and sowre cowntenance, which semyd to savor of mischief, and utter evydently craft and deceyt. The whyle he was thinking of any matter, he dyd continually byte his nether lyppe, as thowgh that crewell nature of his did so rage agaynst ys selfe in that lyttle carkasse.[8]

Vergil sets up a tradition in which Richard's villainy can be read into the signs of his body, especially from the vantage point of his death and the subsequent display of his defeated carcass. And yet, here at the end of Shakespeare's play, the body is reduced practically to detritus, its display somewhat effaced.

Shakespeare's history plays, throughout, put pressure on the moment of succession or, rather, on the moment when the crown is handed over more generally. They stage a series of difficult, even botched, transfers of the crown from one king to the next. From the nobles squabbling over the coffin of Henry V in *Henry VI* part one to Hal's premature seizing of the crown in his father's bedchamber in *Henry IV* part two, succession is not once imagined as the smooth transition of political theory. Even the supposedly legitimate inheritance of his father's throne by Hal/Henry V is marked, in *Henry V*, by anxiety over the legitimacy of his claims. These last moments of *Richard III*, however, might, for all of their Tudor triumphalism, be the most difficult and awkward of all. Richard III has held our attention throughout the play. Of all the history plays, this is the one that seems most to conform to the narrative pattern of a tragedy, with Richard as a central tragic antihero. To have his corpse littering the stage, dishonoured and unremarked upon: one way of reading this situation is simply that it is a necessary corollary to Richmond's ascendancy; another is that it lingers as an all-too material reminder of the violence deployed against the body in the course of constructing sovereign authority, and of the ways that claims to sovereignty are never finished, never absolute.

*Richard III* is, then, the most paradoxical of Shakespeare's history plays. Like *Richard II* and *Henry V*, it features a charismatic central figure. In a reading of the play that I will return to, Andreas Höfele describes Richard as 'the undisputed centre of his own drama'.[9] In the terms that I have been using to think about the narrative focus of the plays, it is clear that the play is centripetal in character, with the action both emerging from and circulating around the figure of Richard himself. However, unlike *Richard II* and *Henry V*, this central figure is in no way, and at no point, understood as a legitimate ruler. In fact, until the final scene in which Richmond claims the crown and ushers in the Tudor dynasty, the play devotes next to no stage-time at all to any claimant to the English crown who might be considered at all legitimate. It is a play that circles around what appears a highly centralised form of sovereignty, in which decisions are made according to the sovereign will of an individual, but where that centre is utterly vacant. Richard is all will, a perverse realisation of a Bodinesque inalienable sovereignty that seeks to inhere in a single body. But the play's concentrated focus on that body leaves any sense of 'majesty' behind. The only scene in which Edward IV, the notionally legitimate king, appears is one in which he announces his impending death, and from which he is carried off stage, too sick to walk. Of course, the young Prince of Wales, Prince Edward, is the supposed heir to the throne when he first appears on stage but, like his father, he exits to his inevitable death, this time in the Tower alongside his cousin. There are questions throughout the Henry IV plays about the legitimacy of Henry's hold on the throne, but that is as nothing to the way in which the illegitimacy of Richard's rule is placed at the centre of this play. If this is a centrifugal play, drawing us into the centres of sovereign power, then that centre is nothing but a vacuum. The play, *Richard III*, is both a study in centralising, decisionist sovereignty and a study of illegitimate rule: 'vacuous / Ceremony of possession, restless / Habitation, no man's resting place'.[10]

Richard is both Shakespeare's most charismatic English king and, in another sense, his most marginal. For all of his appalling violence, he is the most compelling speaker. For all of the strong sense of sovereign will that attaches itself to him – his 'decisionism' and a capacity to promote himself to the crown almost through willing it to happen – there is also a lingering sense of the haphazard and the contingent about his ascent to, and fall from, the throne. Often lost in the more famous call for the horse, Richard also takes time in his last words to describe his life, and his pitch at the crown, as a kind of wager. 'I have set my life upon a cast', he says, 'And I will stand the hazard of the die' (5.6.9–10).[11] These lines, echoing references to gambling that feature elsewhere in the play, operate at the limit point of sovereign will. Richard, as he often does, powerfully asserts his presence and his agency: 'I have set my life upon a cast.' Unlike King John or Henry IV, he has acted on his own behalf, for himself, his actions seemingly comprehensible only as an extension of his peculiar will. But his words also admit of his, and our, dissolution into chaos, into 'hazard'. Games of 'hazard' are played in *Henry V*, when Henry responds to the Dauphin's gift of tennis balls at the start of the play by offering to 'play a set / Shall strike his father's crown into the hazard' (1.2.262–3). Here the 'hazard' is the recipient's half of the court in a game of real tennis. Later, on the eve of Agincourt, the French soldiers joke about betting on the number of prisoners they will take. 'Will you go to hazard with me for twenty prisoners?', asks Rambures. The Constable replies, 'You must first go yourself to hazard, ere you have them' (3.7.70–1). The Dauphin must first stake his life upon the outcome of the battle, before he can claim any prisoners. A suggestion of the contingent and haphazard nature of battle lends yet one more ironic shadow to the picture of Henry as being destined to victory in *Henry V*.

But in *Richard III*, a whole world of contingency is what Richard both creates and fully occupies with the machinations that eventually see him become king.

Some of the ambiguity in Richard's claim to an agency that is, nonetheless, contingent is captured in the sentence from his opening soliloquy, 'I am determined to play the villain' (1.1.30). This statement could either mean that Richard is, himself, resolute in his intentions to behave villainously, or that he has been marked out by fate or some other exterior agency to play that part. Either he has decided to play the villain, or it has been decided that he should play the villain. It is not clear which of these Richard really means, and yet, somewhere between these two seemingly opposite possibilities, Richard improvises his life as a series of wagers. When he makes the audacious, but strategically crucial, move to woo Anne, despite having killed both her husband and her father-in-law, King Henry VI, Richard says that he has managed to win her despite the odds being 'all the world to nothing' (1.2.233). Later, when his plans turn to marrying Elizabeth, the daughter of the former Queen Elizabeth, he acknowledges that if he is unsuccessful in this aim, then 'my kingdom stands on brittle glass', but also that, even if successful, the path that he is taking is an 'Uncertain way of gain' (4.2.60–2). And he projects his potential victories as 'gains' from the very first soliloquy: 'When they [his rivals for the throne] are gone, then must I count my gains' (1.1.160). His achievements are those of a gamester; they are always contingent upon circumstance, even while the form of the play generates all of the action from his centralising presence.

Richard III would love to be a Schmittian sovereign – decisionist, with a will to bend the world to his fantasies – but the world in which he finds himself and which, to a large extent, he does bring into being is beyond his capacity to control. If your decision is a decision to gamble, then you are willing yourself into a situation over which you acknowledge you have no control. His path towards the crown, and his means of maintaining the crown, may well involve decisions in some of the senses meant by Schmitt: extra-judicial, not intended to operate within the normal expectations of a system but in a way that reconfigures the political relationships within which people will work. But to imagine these claims to sovereignty as a wager is to place decisionist absolutism against a dissonant horizon of contingency. Richard's final words are one last gamble: staking his whole kingdom on the possibility of an escape by horse. But by this point, the odds have lengthened beyond his reach. In what follows, I show how this was always going to be the case. The sovereign agency of Shakespeare's most Schmittian king was always curtailed in two ways: through the play's abundant reliance on animal imagery, and through the importance placed by the play on the opposition of women to Richard's rise. In both of these aspects of the play, Richard's seeming decisionism is pulled apart. Or, rather, it never was anything more than an empty wager.

## Richard III: Sovereign or Beast?

Outside the two forest-bound comedies, *A Midsummer Night's Dream* and *As You Like It*, and the feral *Titus Andronicus*, it would be hard to think of a more creaturely play than *Richard III*. Metaphors and similes that depend upon comparisons of Richard with various animals proliferate throughout the dialogue. For the most part, these are attempts to describe the extraordinary monstrosity of Richard's villainy in terms that place him outside the human, with the most common insult being to refer to him as a hog, boar or pig, referencing his coat-of-arms. But more is at stake in these comparisons than an extended gloss on More's description of Richard as a 'cur dogge'.

Derrida's discussion of links between sovereignty and animality in *The Sovereign and the Beast* is, in part, an extended consideration of the Latin proverb, *homo homini lupus* ('Man is a wolf to man'). One of the ways in which Derrida exposes the fallacy of sovereign ipseity, of the singular will, is to subject the idea of man as 'political animal' to rigorous analysis, and to reveal animality at the origin of sovereign will. The prosthstatics that shadow claims to sovereign agency, as analysed in relation to the hand in the earlier chapter on *King John*, can also be thought through in relation to an idea of the animal or, more properly, the 'beast', a figure that is already figured as part human/part animal in so much as it is drawn within an anthropocentric moral compass. 'The beast is the sovereign who is the beast', Derrida writes, 'both sharing ... a being outside-the-law, above or at a distance from the laws.'[12] Richard III is, in the language of the play, more beast than man, a 'wolf' to man.

The emblematic event that confirms Richard's tyranny is the murder of the young princes in the Tower. In response to this, Queen Elizabeth rails against a God who has allowed it to happen and names Richard as the devouring wolf:

> Wilt thou, O God, fly from such gentle lambs
> And throw them in the entrails of the wolf?
> When didst thou sleep when such a deed was done? (4.4.22–4)

This is the only time that Richard is directly compared to a wolf, but this is just one of the many animals with which he is associated or to which he is compared, including various kinds of dog. In the same scene, the old queen, Queen Margaret, takes this particular comparison to an extreme as she rails against the other women, particularly Richard's mother, the Duchess of York:

> From forth the kennel of thy womb hath crept
> A hell-hound that doth hunt us all to death.
> That dog that had his teeth before his eyes,
> To worry lambs and lap their gentle blood;
> That foul defacer of God's handiwork,
> That reigns in gallèd eyes of weeping souls;
> That excellent grand tyrant of the earth,
> Thy womb let loose, to chase us to our graves. (4.4.47–54)

The comparison to a 'cur dogge' in Thomas More's account of Richard's ignominious end is extended throughout Shakespeare's play. And while this speech might be particularly extreme, as well as gloriously virtuosic in its anger, it epitomises the beast-laden dialogue that runs throughout the play.

In some ways, the dialogue of *Richard III* offers just as much of a lesson in *copia* as the *Henry IV* plays, with their incessant, bloated lists. But the copiousness of *Richard III* all stems from a particular area: an incredible proliferation of animals. Höfele explains Richard as associated, in part, with a kind of multiplicity: 'Evolving multiple personalities, Richard branches out into multiple animal personae as well. Proteus and chameleon are the twin patrons of his self-creation.'[13] There is an unremarked irony, however, in the idea of Richard as 'self-created'. While it is true that he seeks to assert a form of self-generated sovereignty (ipseity), the manifold animality with which he becomes associated would tend to dissipate any such 'self-creation'. 'Hedgehog', 'toad', 'packhorse', 'abortive, rooting hog' and 'bottled spider': these are among the many animals to which he is compared during the course of the play, both by others and by himself. Richard is a one-man menagerie. Just as in the *Henry IV* plays, the copiousness of Shakespeare's language, its tendency towards fecund multiplication, could be said to resist the restriction of sovereign agency to a singular person. Höfele writes that Richard's multiplicity makes him a 'perfect mirror for majesty', but I do not think that this is quite right. 'Majesty' as an idea or as a word is closely connected to concepts of sovereignty that see it as inalienable, and that would sit uneasily within these more metamorphic formations. The body of sovereign majesty is unitary, not multiple. Höfele is, I think, closer to what is happening in the play when he describes 'Richard's radical individualism . . . severed from the social and dynastic organism that should support it'.[14] This 'radical individualism' I would understand as an unsustainable fantasy of ipseity, the imaginary nature of which is exposed throughout the play.

Considering work done within the field of early modern human/animal studies, Richard's individualism – his exceptionalism – might be seen both in the context of, and against the grain of, an expanded sense of agency that is not restricted to the category of the human at all. The copious plurality of *Richard III*'s animals partakes in the political culture that Laurie Shannon describes as open to the possibility of agency not being limited solely to the human. Shakespeare's creaturely language she associates with a world of 'legitimated capacities, authorities, and rights that set animals within the scope of justice and the span of political imagination'.[15] The distinction between human and animal is not, yet, in the early modern world, so clearly defined as it would come to be in the following centuries. This is partly made apparent by the lack of reference to a singular, generic 'animal', in contradistinction to a category of the 'human', in Shakespeare, notwithstanding his copiously zoological texts:

> There were creatures. There were brutes, and there were beasts. There were fish and fowl. There were living things. There were humans who participated in 'animal nature' and experienced the same material and humoral conditions of life as animals did.[16]

Derrida's 'beast', 'a being outside-the-law, above or at a distance from the laws', is not quite the same as Shannon's multiple brutes and beasts, creatures that, for us, undermine any claims to specifically human exceptionalism through their apparent participation in a political community, within 'the scope of justice'.[17] With Richard, we see, however, paradoxical claims to exceptionalism being made on the basis of his proximity to, or participation in, forms of the 'beast'. This exceptionalism unravels as the copiousness of Shakespeare's language, associated with the irrepressible variety of early modern creatureliness, takes over. That this, in the play, is very clearly gendered is also something that works against the centripetal energies of Richard's peculiar claims to exceptional status.

## Richard III's Exceptionalism

At the start of his play, Richard begins by seeming to be part of a broader political tribe or community. 'Now is the winter of *our* discontent', he opens, 'Made glorious summer by these sons of York' (1.1.1–2). It is the shared success of the House of York over the House of Lancaster that he starts by celebrating. This continues for a mere twelve lines, three of which begin anaphoristically with 'Our': 'Our bruisèd arms', 'Our stern alarums', 'Our dreadful marches' (1.1.6–8). However, the famous opening speech comes with a famous 'but': 'But I that am not shaped for sportive tricks' (1.1.14). Richard never looks back and, from this moment on, it is mostly all 'I'. In the other plays, Richard II vacillates between pronouns, producing a confused representation of sovereign agency, and Henry V alternates shiftily between 'I' and 'we', as he tries to shift the terms upon which he might be held responsible for his own decisions. Richard III at times does this, although his assumption of the royal 'we' appears more like self-aggrandisement than blame shifting. However, Richard's first-person opening account of himself – 'I that am' – inaugurates a tendency towards a self-generated will from which he never deviates, even as it is revealed as unsustainable. Moreover, he bases his exceptionalism on his particular body. His is an inalienable exceptionalism that inheres in the particular body of the (at this stage would-be) king:

> I that am rudely stamped, and want love's majesty
> To strut before a wanton-ambling nymph;
> I that am cùrtailed of this fair proportion,
> Cheated of feature by dissembling nature,
> Deformed, unfinished, sent before my time
> Into this breathing world scarce half made up,
> And that so lamely and unfashionable
> That dogs bark at me as I halt by them—
> Why, I in this weak-piping time of peace
> Have no delight to pass away the time,
> Unless to see my shadow in the sun
> And descant on mine own deformity. (1.1.16–27)

It may be that he lacks '*love's* majesty', but the claim to a certain form of majesty remains. And even though Richard claims to have been sent 'Into this breathing world scarce half made up', the overall drive of his character is towards an assumption of total self-reliance.

This is made evident throughout the play by his gradual sloughing off of conspirators, allies and counsellors. First to go is Hastings. 'Now my lord', Buckingham asks, 'what shall we do if we perceive / Lord Hastings will not yield to our complots?' (3.1.190–1). 'Chop off his head', comes the straightforward reply from Richard, following it up with, 'Something we will determine' (3.1.192). That is, he will find reasons after the event (and here he does use the royal 'we' that Henry V also uses for authorising executions) to justify the execution that he has already decided upon. These *post hoc* explanations perfectly encapsulate the decisionism that Richard claims as his right. Sovereignty, for Richard, comes very clearly before the law, even though he does pay lip service to legal precedent. When Lovell presents the head of the executed Hastings, Richard feigns regret while claiming to have acted according to the law:

> What, think you we are Turks or infidels,
> Or that we would, against the form of law,
> Proceed thus rashly in the villain's death,
> But that the èxtreme peril of the case,
> The peace of England, and our persons' safety,
> Enforced us to this executïon? (3.5.41–6)

Even though Richard is claiming to act on behalf of the law, or within the compass of the law, this moment is, as it turns out, a high point for his capacity to act according to his will. And it is to be noted that he equates 'the peace of England' with the safety of his own 'person'. The simple 'Chop off his head' sees the act done within the space of moments, and Richard's claims to have acted legally appear, in the end, more like threats to the mayor of London, who is present when Lovell brings in Hastings' severed head, than the words of somebody who really feels the need to exempt himself through reference to due process. As Höfele writes, it is the axe that makes space for Richard's exceptionalism:

> Carving out his kingship from the flesh of foes, friends, and kin, the bloody axe becomes the concrete image of Richard's total self-isolation, his severing of all family ties ... The sign of the axe thus comes to hover over the singular state of the king as conceived by the terms of Richard's radical individualism: it makes the head of state bodiless, severed from the social and dynastic organism that should support it.[18]

Howard and Rackin agree, writing that 'He eschews all kinship ties; he relies on his theatrical skills and his seductive charm to attain his ends.'[19] Lone wolf, and leading player in his own drama, Richard continues along this route with the killing of Buckingham, although he is eventually unable to continue in this 'bodiless' state; his final calls for a horse signal his ultimate lack of self-reliance. But already in the story of Buckingham, we see glimpses of this as well. He is never able to command in quite the way that he does with Hastings' death.

Buckingham's fall from favour originates with his seeming incapacity to act according to Richard's will without having to be told. In a scene that appears, at first, to be like those scenes in *King John* in which John insinuates his murderous plot against Prince Arthur's life to Hubert, Richard tries to imply that the princes in the Tower should be killed. He doesn't want to say anything out loud, but Buckingham is deliberately obtuse, and Richard ends up having to 'be plain' about his desire to see the young princes murdered:

> KING RICHARD Ah, Buckingham, now do I play the touch,
> To try if thou be current gold indeed.
> Young Edward lives. Think now what I would speak.
> BUCKINGHAM Say on, my loving lord.
> KING RICHARD Why, Buckingham, I say I would be king.
> BUCKINGHAM Why so you are, my thrice-renownèd lord.
> KING RICHARD Ha, am I king? 'Tis so; but Edward lives.
> BUCKINGHAM True, noble prince.
> KING RICHARD                    O bitter consequence:
> That Edward still should live 'true noble prince'.
> Cousin, thou wast not wont to be so dull.
> Shall I be plain? I wish the bastards dead,
> And I would have it suddenly performed. (4.2.8–19)

Richard's attempts to convey his sovereign will are initially very similar to those of King John, 'Without a tongue, using conceit alone' (3.3.50).[20] And, like Elizabeth I to parliament when she says, 'If I should say that I would do it, it were not fit in this place and at this time', Richard is eager for his will to be simply known without him being forced to articulate it, or to take responsibility for the actions that result.[21] Buckingham's obtuseness, as he refuses to follow Richard's heavy-handed hints, renders him useless in Richard's increasingly exceptionalist model of sovereignty. For Richard, Buckingham should not be afforded the space to make his own mind up about the validity of any action. As the editors of the *New Oxford Shakespeare* edition point out, it is often from this moment onwards that the actor performing the role of Richard appears increasingly nervous or out of control. Buckingham resists being co-opted as a near-telepathic extension of Richard's will and, as a result, his time is up. He recognises his own role in producing Richard as king, and later sees his own fate presaged by that of Hastings:

> Made I him king for this?
> O, let me think on Hastings and be gone
> To Brecknock while my fearful head is on. (4.2.118–20)

However, Richard cannot work without any deputies at all, and he whispers his instructions to Tyrrell who says, 'I will dispatch it straight' (4.2.80). Immediately in the scene following, we learn that the murders were in fact carried out, in turn, by two men 'suborned' by Tyrrell:

> The tyrannous and bloody act is done,
> The most arch-deed of piteous massacre
> That ever yet this land was guilty of.
> Dighton and Forrest, who I did suborn
> To do this piece of ruthful butchery—
> Albeit they were fleshed villains, bloody dogs—

Melted with tenderness and mild compassion,
Wept like two children in their deaths' sad story. (4.3.1–8)

'Suborn' is a word that originates in legal contexts in the mid-sixteenth century and its tone of technical expertise makes a startling contrast with the phrase, 'piece of butchery'. What follows, in Tyrrell's soliloquy, is a powerful, ekphrastic account of the death of the two young princes. But it is an account at second or even third hand, as Tyrrell reports to the audience what has been reported to him by his 'bloody dogs'; it is a report of a report which is, itself, the verbal translation of a startling visual scene. At the heart of Richard's decisionism is a paradoxical, but inevitable secondariness, a dependence on deputisation, on 'suborning'.

The apotheosis of Richard's impossible retreat into himself comes between the visitation of the ghosts and the beginning of the battle of Bosworth. And here, Richard's crazed rhetoric evidences the fantastical nature of his solipsism:

> Richard loves Richard, that is, I and I.
> Is there a murderer here? No. – Yes, I am.
> Then fly. – What from myself? – Great reason. – Why? –
> Lest I revenge. – What, myself upon myself?
> Alack, I love myself. – Wherefore? For any good
> That I myself have done unto myself?
> O no. Alas, I rather hate myself,
> For hateful deeds committed by myself.
> I am a villain. – Yet I lie, I am not. (5.4.163–71)

The cracks that appear in Richard's speech at this point prefigure similar forms in the self-generated madness of Leontes in *The Winter's Tale*. The ambiguities and paradoxes of his opening gambit – 'I am determined to play the villain' – have now fallen apart: 'I am a villain. – Yet I lie, I am not.' Or, as Derrida would put it, a sovereignty that is 'said and supposed to be indivisible but [which is] always divisible'.[22]

## 'This it is when men are ruled by women'

For the most part, Richard's animal comparisons see him as vicious: a wild hog, a tiger or a wolfish dog. Other animal comparisons, however, draw closer attention to his physical disability, characterising him as not upright, as being unable to stand up properly, hooped and downwards-looking: a 'bottled spider' and a 'bunch-backed toad' (1.3.241; 1.3.245). Even when he is characterised as a more fearful animal than a toad or a spider, he is still often imagined as downwards-looking, rooting around in the viscera of his prey: revelling, as Queen Elizabeth puts it, 'in the entrails of my lambs' (4.4.229). His lack of an upright posture links him still closer to the animal world and, as Shannon points out, sees him potentially excluded from being considered 'human' at all. Some early modern writers considered human exceptionalism and, by extension, their capacity and right to rule as derived from their uniquely upright stance. Within this mindset, Shannon writes, 'To be crooked and bent with a downcast look is to have bowing submission spelled out in one's body', and she quotes a passage from Golding's translation of the *Metamorphoses* where he contrasts the way that beasts 'behold the ground with groveling eie' with Man's 'stately looke replete with majestie'.[23] Something that might undergird human, and therefore sovereign, exceptionalism – 'majestie' – is denied to Richard, and yet it is precisely on these grounds – his unique and solitary difference from others – that he pitches his own form of exceptionalism. Shannon goes on to illustrate the multiple ways in which these claims to upright, bipedal exceptionalism were a 'high-maintenance proposition' that often proved unsustainable as grounds to figure the difference between human and non-human animals.[24] Nevertheless, these categories are in operation in *Richard III*, and Richard III appears as a king whose body instantiates a form of sovereignty that is in marked contrast to Richard II's claims to 'The unstooping firmness of my upright soul' (1.1.121) at the beginning of *Richard II*.

There is, in fact, a particular masculinist verticality to the way that Richard II is sometimes characterised in the later play, something that is only really undone when he is forced to descend from the castle walls at Flint: 'Down, down I come, like glistering Phaëton, / Wanting the manage of unruly jades' (3.3.177–8). At this point, like Richard III at Bosworth, Richard II is imagined as unable to control his horses. 'Manage' here is a technical term for properly trained horsemanship, the masterful control over horses (and, by implication, other animals including human animals) that would otherwise be 'unruly'. Most glosses will point out that the metaphorical use of 'jade', a word for an inferior horse, is being contemptuously targeted by Richard against his own noblemen. But 'jade' is also a term for a prostitute or, at least, a word used by men to describe a woman whom they consider to be 'unruly'. And right from the start of *his* play, Richard III has problems asserting his rule in relation to women.

In the opening scene, not long after he has made his statement of perverse exceptionalism – 'determinèd to prove a villain' – Richard is disingenuously commiserating with his brother, Clarence, who has been arrested by King Edward. We learn that this arrest was largely the result of Richard's own intervention, but he gives Clarence quite different reasons:

> Why, this it is when men are ruled by women.
> 'Tis not the King that sends you to the Tower.
> My Lady Grey, his wife, Clarence, 'tis she
> That tempts him to this harsh extremity. (1.1.62–5)

By the end of that opening scene Clarence is despatched to the Tower, but it is the very next scene that witnesses Richard's wooing of Lady Anne. Howard and Rackin rightly emphasise the theatricality of Richard's performance and the way that this theatricality 'invites the audience to suspend their moral judgement and evaluate his actions simply as theatrical performances'.[25] We, they argue, are seduced against our better judgement in just the way that Anne is during this scene. Howard and Rackin's point is part of a much broader argument that rightly sees the agency of women curtailed as Shakespeare's history plays move on. It is undeniable that figures such as Queen Margaret and Joan of Arc from the *Henry VI* plays are much more powerful presences than the domesticated Princess Katharine in *Henry V*. And here, in *Richard III*, they make the important point that Princess Elizabeth, the key figure in the dynastic success of Richmond and the Tudor family, does not even appear in the play. When, in his final speech, Richmond declares, 'We will unite the white rose and the red' (5.7.19), that is a royal 'we' that he is using; he is not speaking as a married couple. And when both he and the play conclude, 'peace lives again. / That she may long live here, God say "amen"' (5.7.40–1), there is a distinct reordering of gendered priorities. It is not to be thought, now, that Richmond would ever 'want the manage of unruly jades', or allow himself to be 'ruled by women'.

For all that this argument is compelling, I think that there are two ways in which claims to an exceptional masculinist sovereignty might be open to question in the language and action of this play. The chorus of women who punctuate the play's action open out an alternate location of power that is not easily sidestepped either by Richard's seductive performance or by Richmond's dynastic marriage. And the source of Richard's claims to his peculiar, isolated exceptionalism – his animality or beastliness – is, throughout the play, particularly associated with women. Moreover, the Tudor future to which the play looks forward is one that is characterised by a dynasty of successive women, including the incumbent Elizabeth I. As I have been arguing, the focus on the increasingly isolated central figure of Richard in this play reveals the specious nature of any claims to sovereign exceptionalism, in as much as those claims are founded on the indivisible body of the king, on 'majesty'. One way of figuring this is through the peculiarly secondary nature of Richard's supposed solitude – his dependence on deputies and then, finally, on that 'horse'. Another is through the gendered implications of his claims to self-sufficiency.

Moving from his feigned complaint that Edward IV is overly dependent on the queen for the decisions that he makes, the 'wooing' scene potentially sees Richard reassert some kind of masculinist privilege. And yet, for all that his performance is virtuosic, there are also moments when the whole thing seems rather anxious. In particular, Richard's sense of who he is seems, at times, not so self-sufficient as he would like but, rather, dependent on the way that he is reflected back by Anne:

> And will she yet abase her eyes on me,
> That cropped the golden prime of this sweet prince
> And made her widow to a woeful bed?
> On me, whose all not equals Edward's moiety?
> On me, that halts, and am misshapen thus?
> My dukedom to a beggarly denier,
> I do mistake my person all this while.
> Upon my life, she finds – although I cannot –
> Myself to be a marv'lous proper man.
> I'll be at charges for a looking-glass,
> And entertain a score or two of tailors
> To study fashions to adorn my body.
> Since I am crept in favour with myself,
> I will maintain it with some little cost. (1.2.242–55)

Although, of course, this is all false modesty, and Richard is not being anything other than disingenuous, there is still a strong sense that he is, somehow, no longer like himself, no longer self-sufficient, no longer 'determined' but, rather, dependent, in his relationship with Anne. The adding up and calculation of worth – 'whose all not equals Edward's moiety' – undermines the sense of Richard as singular, as a lone wolf. And again, he seems to take a gamble on his status: 'My dukedom to a beggarly denier, / I do mistake my person all this while.' Just as he is willing, later on, to pawn his kingdom for a horse, he briefly entertains the idea that he might chance his dukedom against the stake of a mere denier (a coin of little value) on having misunderstood himself. The scene that is sometimes taken as the epitome of Richard's self-validating claims to an absolutist sovereignty, or mastery of those around him, concludes with at least some sense of his identity being dissipated through the contingency of misjudged values and, particularly perhaps, his dependence on the judgement of women.

The very next scene begins with the complaints of the queen that her husband, King Edward, is about to die. And while this is, of course, a portrait of a woman who is dependent on her husband for what status she has, it does inaugurate a succession of scenes in which Richard's rule is subject to critique from women, reaching a climax in Queen Margaret's attacks on the Duchess of York, as Richard's mother. Her description of the duchess's womb as a 'kennel' that gives birth to a 'hell-hound' echoes something that the duchess has already said herself:

> O my accursèd womb, the bed of death,
> A cockatrice hast thou hatched to the world
> Whose unavoided eye is murderous. (4.1.53–5)

Both of these speeches participate in a misogynist language of 'monstrous birth' in which the production of horrors is imputed to women's responsibility for reproduction and childbirth. But at the same time, it gives the lie to Richard's monstrosity as something that underpins his isolated exceptionalism.

Richard, then, like all of Shakespeare's kings, is caught within the complexities of dynastic struggle and inheritance, complexities that, even as they attempt to inhere sovereignty into the majestic bodies of kings, reveal the origins of sovereign agency as always multiple. When Richmond closes the play, he makes some claims about the ways in which his marriage will confirm the success of the Tudor dynasty. But he does this over the mangled body of Richard III, his corpse either still on stage or having been unceremoniously lugged off. And Richard has already, in the play, given us a much darker picture of dynastic claims to the throne. Having killed Anne, he now wants to marry Princess Elizabeth and is persuading her mother, Queen Elizabeth, to act on his behalf. Richard admits that he has treated her, up to this point, as his enemy, taking the crown from her sons:

> If I did take the kingdom from your sons,
> To make amends I'll give it to your daughter.
> If I have killed the issue of your womb,
> To quicken your increase I will beget
> Mine issue of your blood upon your daughter.
> A grandam's name is little less in love
> Than is the doting title of a mother.
> They are as children but one step below,
> Even of your mettle, of your very blood;
> Of all one pain, save for a night of groans
> Endured of her for whom you bid like sorrow.
> Your children were vexation to your youth,
> But mine shall be a comfort to your age.
> The loss you have is but a son being king,
> And by that loss your daughter is made queen. (4.4.294–308)

Richard's offer is, frankly, horrific. It is the image of a royal family consuming itself. The repair of the kingdom that Richard is planning is dependent on something very close to incest, as the queen is being asked to accept the replacement of her sons by Richard who wishes to marry her daughter. This image of a dynasty that is collapsing in on itself is the dark shadow of Richmond's sunny optimism.

There are two ways in which early modern sovereignty could seek to repair the inevitable fissures in the claims made for its self-authorising power. One would be a Bodinesque argument that any forms of deputisation, any dispersals of authority beyond the majestic body of the unitary sovereign, were only ever notional. In *Richard III*, as in other of Shakespeare's history plays and particularly in *King John*, the idea that as the sovereign deputises, 'he never gives so much that he does not hold back even more' is revealed as entirely unsustainable.[26] Richard's decisionism, his attempts to impose his determined will on those around him, never works in any other way than to dissipate his claims to sovereignty. His isolation gradually increases throughout the play until the moment that he is horseless and desperately unable to act at all. The other way is through the principle of dynastic continuance. And while, as an aspect of Tudor propaganda, the play does seem to underline the validity of this, there is also a strong current in the play that sees the wombs of queens as kennels for wolfish dogs. In both these aspects, *Richard III* puts forward one of Shakespeare's most thorough demonstrations of the contingencies of sovereignty.

## Notes

1. Geoffrey Hill, 'Funeral Music', in *Broken Hierarchies: Poems 1952–2012*, ed. Kenneth Haynes (Oxford: Oxford University Press, 2013), p. 47.
2. Polydore Vergil, *Three Books of Polydore Vergil's English History*, ed. Sir Henry Ellis (London: Camden Society, 1844), p. 226. Ellis's edition is an of early manuscript translation of Vergil.
3. Thomas More, *The History of King Richard III*, ed. George M. Logan (Indianapolis: Indiana University Press, 2005), p. 102.
4. Philip Schwyzer, *Shakespeare and the Remains of Richard III* (Oxford: Oxford University Press, 2013), p. 20.
5. Schwyzer, *Shakespeare and the Remains of Richard III*, p. 20.
6. William Shakespeare, *Richard III* (3rd Arden edn), ed. James R. Siemon (London: Methuen, 2009), 5.5.1.sd.n.
7. Greta Olson, 'Richard III's Animalistic Criminal Body', *Philological Quarterly* 82.3 (2003), p. 303.
8. Vergil, *Three Books of Polydore Vergil's English History*, p. 227.
9. Andreas Höfele, *Stage, Stake, and Scaffold: Humans and Animals*

    *in Shakespeare's Theatre* (Oxford: Oxford University Press, 2011), p. 69.
10. Hill, 'Funeral Music', p. 47. Geoffrey Hill's astonishing sonnet sequence is concerned, in the first instance, with the executions of three Yorkists during the Wars of the Roses, including Tiptoft, the 'butcher of England', and, ultimately, with the illegitimacy of state-sanctioned or religiously justified violence. The final lines of the second sonnet capture the tone of bitter resentment that punctuates the sequence: 'Recall the cold / Of Towton on Palm Sunday before dawn, / Wakefield, Tewkesbury: fastidious trumpets / Shrilling into the ruck; some trampled / Acres, parched, sodden or blanched by sleet, / Stuck with strange-postured dead. Recall the wind's / Flurrying, darkness over the human mire.'
11. Shakespeare likes jokes about death, gambling and the ends of plays. At the end of his spectacularly awful performance as Pyramus in front of the Athenian court, Bottom, in *A Midsummer Night's Dream* cries, 'Now die, die, die, die', as he dies (5.1.291). The snobbish audience take this as a cue to make jokes at his expense: 'No die but an ace for him; for he is but one', Demetrius comments, with puns on die/die (plural of dice) and ace/ ass. Lysander piles on: 'Less than an ace, man, for he is dead; he is nothing' (292). The potential pathos of the line, 'he is nothing', is mitigated by Theseus's interjection that Bottom might yet prove an ass by, with the help of a surgeon, coming back to life. This is, I suppose, a million miles away from Richard's desperation, but there are some commonalities: an understanding of the ends of both death and tragedy being somehow contingent if they are reconceived as a gamble, a game of 'hazard'.
12. Derrida, *The Beast and the Sovereign*, vol. I, p. 70.
13. Höfele, *Stage, State, and Scaffold*, p. 90.
14. Höfele, *Stage, State, and Scaffold*, p. 76.
15. Laurie Shannon, *The Accommodated Animal: Cosmopolity in Shakespeare's Locales* (Chicago: University of Chicago Press, 2013), p. 3.
16. Shannon, *The Accommodated Animal*, p. 10.
17. The most obvious example of this being the case is the existence of the notorious animal trials, mostly popular in France, and covered by Shannon in her book. But this participation would also extend to the ways in which the 'animal' is brought within what Keith Thomas would call 'the same moral universe' inhabited by both early modern 'men and beasts'; Keith Thomas, *Man and the Natural World: Changing Attitudes in England 1500–1800* (Harmondsworth: Penguin, 1983), p. 99. Höfele's work, cited above, also considers the shared polity of men and beasts through what he calls the 'intermediality' of the bear-pit, the theatre and the execution scaffold (Höfele, *Stage, State, and Scaffold*, p. 13). This latter derives from Erica Fudge's account of early modern bear-baiting which she reads as an event in which an attempt to establish distinctions between species flounders on shared understandings of both violence and personal agency. The bears appear to have characteristics that are potentially 'human', where the human participants' capacity for cruelty reveals them to be bestially violent: 'The violence involved in taming wild nature – in expressing human superiority – destroys the difference between the species'; Erica Fudge, *Perceiving Animals: Humans and Beasts in Early Modern English Culture* (London: Palgrave, 2000), p. 19.

18. Höfele, *Stage, State, and Scaffold*, p. 76.
19. Howard and Rackin, *Engendering a Nation*, p. 114.
20. This similarity is pointed out in Siemon's notes to the third Arden edition of the play, with a further comparison also made with the scene in which Bolingbroke, once he is crowned as Henry IV, insinuates to Sir Piers Exton his requirement that Richard II be murdered (4.2.5–17n.).
21. Elizabeth I, *Collected Works*, p. 199.
22. Derrida, *The Beast and the Sovereign*, vol. I, p. 291.
23. Shannon, *The Accommodated Animal*, pp. 88–9.
24. Shannon, *The Accommodated Animal*, p. 93.
25. Howard and Rackin, *Engendering a Nation*, p. 111.
26. Bodin, *On Sovereignty*, p. 2.

# Bibliography

Agamben, Giorgio, *Homo Sacer: Sovereign Power and Bare Life*, trans. Daniel Heller-Roazen (Stanford: Stanford University Press, 1998).
—, *The Kingdom and the Glory: For a Theological Genealogy of Economy and Government*, trans. Lorenzo Chiesa (Stanford: Stanford University Press, 2011).
—, *State of Exception*, trans. Kevin Attell (Chicago: University of Chicago Press, 2005).
Anderson, Thomas, '"Legitimation, name, and all is gone": Bastardy and Bureaucracy in Shakespeare's *King John*', *Journal for Early Modern Cultural Studies* 4 (2004), pp. 35–61.
Anonymous, *The First part of the Contention betwixt the two famous Houses of Yorke and Lancaster* (London, 1594).
Aravamudan, Srinivas, 'Subjects/Sovereigns/Rogues', *Eighteenth-Century Studies* 40.3 (2007), pp. 457–65, special issue, 'Derrida's Eighteenth Century'.
Archer, John Michael, *Sovereignty and Intelligence: Spying and Court Culture in the English Renaissance* (Stanford: Stanford University Press, 1995).
Bate, Jonathan, *Shakespeare and Ovid* (Oxford: Oxford University Press, 1993).
Benjamin, Walter, *The Origin of German Tragic Drama*, trans. John Osborne (London: Verso, 1998).
Berger Jr, Harry, *Harrying: Skills of Offence in Shakespeare's* Henriad (New York: Fordham University Press, 2015).
—, *Making Trifles of Terrors: Redistributing Complicities in Shakespeare* (Stanford: Stanford University Press, 1997).
Berry, Ralph, 'Metamorphoses of the Stage', *Shakespeare Quarterly* 33.1 (1982), pp. 5–16.
Bertram, Benjamin, 'Falstaff's Body, the Body Politic, and the Body of Trade', *Exemplaria* 21.3 (2009), pp. 296–318.
Bodin, Jean, *On Sovereignty: Four Chapters from The Six Books of the Commonwealth*, ed. and trans. Julian H. Franklin (Cambridge: Cambridge University Press, 1992).
Bosman, Anton, 'Seeing Tears: Truth and Sense in *All is True*', *Shakespeare Quarterly* 50.4 (1999), pp. 459–76.
Campbell, Lily, 'Shakespeare's Histories: Mirrors of Elizabethan Policy', *The American Historical Review* 52.4 (1947), pp. 725–7.

Cave, Terence, *The Cornucopian Text: Problems of Writing in the French Renaissance* (Oxford: Oxford University Press, 1985).
Cicero, *On the Ideal Orator [de Oratore]*, trans. James M. May and Jakob Wisse (Oxford: Oxford University Press, 2001).
Cohen, Jeffrey Jerome, 'Stories of Stone', *post-medieval* 1.1/2 (2010), pp. 56–63.
Collinson, Patrick, 'The Monarchical Republic of Elizabeth I', *Bulletin of the John Rylands University Library of Manchester* 69.2 (1987), pp. 394–424.
Conti, Brooke, 'The Mechanical Saint: Early Modern Devotion and the Language of Automation', in Wendy Beth Hyman (ed.), *The Automaton in English Renaissance Literature* (Farnham: Ashgate, 2011), pp. 95–107.
Cooper, Farah Karim, *The Hand on the Shakespearean Stage: Gesture, Touch, and the Spectacle of Dismemberment* (London: Bloomsbury, 2016).
Cormack, Bradin, 'Shakespeare's Other Sovereignty: on Particularity and Violence in *The Winter's Tale* and the Sonnets', *Shakespeare Quarterly* 62.4 (2011), pp. 485–513.
Craig, Hugh, 'The Three Parts of *Henry VI*', in Hugh Craig and Arthur Kinney (eds), *Shakespeare, Computers, and the Mystery of Authorship* (Cambridge: Cambridge University Press, 2012), pp. 40–77.
Crawford, Nicholas, 'The Discourse of Dilution in *2 Henry IV*', *Renaissance Papers* (2002), pp. 61–76.
Defoe, Daniel, *Robinson Crusoe*, ed. John Richetti (Harmondsworth: Penguin, 2001).
Deleuze, Gilles, *The Fold: Leibniz and the Baroque*, trans. Tom Conley (Minneapolis: University of Minnesota Press, 1993).
Dening, Greg, 'Performing on the Beaches of the Mind: An Essay', *History and Theory* 41.1 (2002), pp. 1–24.
Derrida, Jacques, *The Beast and the Sovereign*, volume I, ed. Michel Lisse, Marie-Louise Mallet and Ginette Michaud, trans. Geoffrey Bennington (Chicago: University of Chicago Press, 2009),
—, *The Beast and the Sovereign*, volume II, ed. Michel Lisse, Marie-Louise Mallet and Ginette Michaud, trans. Geoffrey Bennington (Chicago: University of Chicago Press, 2010).
—, *The Death Penalty*, volume I, ed. Geoffrey Bennington, Marc Crépon and Thomas Dutoit, trans. Peggy Kamuf (Chicago: University of Chicago Press, 2014).
—, *Rogues: Two Essays on Reason*, trans. Pascale-Anne Brault and Michael Naas (Stanford: Stanford University Press, 2005).
Donne, John, *Devotions Upon Emergent Occasions*, ed. Anthony Raspa (Oxford: Oxford University Press, 1987).
Elam, Keir, *The Semiotics of Theatre and Drama* (London: Routledge, 1980).
Elizabeth I, *Collected Works*, ed. Leah S. Marcus, Janel Mueller and Mary Beth Rose (Chicago: University of Chicago Press, 2000).
Elyot, Thomas, *The Book Named the Governour* (London, 1531).
Enterline, Lynn, *The Rhetoric of the Body from Ovid to Shakespeare* (Cambridge: Cambridge University Press, 2004).
Erasmus, Desidirius, *Literary and Educational Writings Volume 2: de Copia*, ed. Craig R. Thompson (Toronto: University of Toronto Press, 2016).
Erne, Lukas, *Shakespeare as Literary Dramatist* (Cambridge: Cambridge University Press, 2003).

Forker, Charles R., 'Introduction', in William Shakespeare, *King Richard II*, ed. Charles R. Forker (London: Cengage, 2002), pp. 1–164.

Forsett, Edward, *A Comparative Discourse of the Bodies Natural and Politique wherein out of the Principles of Nature, is set forth the True Forme of a Commonweale, with the Dutie of Subiects, and Right of Soveraigne: together with many Good Points of Politicall Learning, mentioned in a Briefe after the Preface* (London, 1606).

Foucault, Michel, *The Birth of Biopolitics: Lectures at the Collège de France*, trans. Graham Burchill (London: Palgrave, 2008).

—, *The Order of Things: An Archaeology of the Human Sciences* (London: Routledge, 1970).

—, *'Society Must Be Defended': Lectures at the Collège de France 1975–1976*, trans. David Macey (New York: Picador, 2003).

Franklin, Julian, *Jean Bodin and the Rise of Absolutism* (Cambridge: Cambridge University Press, 1973).

Fudge, Erica, *Perceiving Animals: Humans and Beasts in Early Modern English Culture* (London: Palgrave, 2000).

Gajda, Alexandra, 'Political Culture in the 1590s: The "Second Reign" of Elizabeth', *History Compass* 8.1 (2010), pp. 88–100.

Gieskes, Edward, '"He is but a Bastard to the Time": Status and Service in *The Troublesome Raigne of John* and Shakespeare's *King John*', *ELH* 65 (1998), pp. 779–98.

Gil, Daniel Juan, *Shakespeare's Anti-Politics: Sovereign Power and the Life of the Flesh* (New York: Palgrave Macmillan, 2013).

Goldberg, Jonathan, *Hamlet's Hand* (Minneapolis: University of Minnesota Press, 2002).

—, *Writing Matter: From the Hands of the English Renaissance* (Stanford: Stanford University Press, 1991).

Grady, Hugh, *John Donne and Baroque Allegory* (Cambridge: Cambridge University Press, 2017).

Greene, Roland, *Five Words: Critical Semantics in the Age of Shakespeare and Cervantes* (Chicago: University of Chicago Press, 2013).

Griffiths, Huw, 'Hotel Rooms and Bodily Fluids in Two Recent Productions of *Measure for Measure*, Or, Why Barnardine is Still Important', *Shakespeare Bulletin* 32.4 (2014), pp. 559–83.

Grudin, Robert, 'Liberty of Ideas: Renaissance Copia and the Nature of Free Thought', *Writing on the Edge* 5.1 (1993), pp. 25–39.

Guy, John, 'Introduction: the 1590s: The Second Reign of Elizabeth I?', in John Guy (ed.), *The Reign of Elizabeth I: Court and Culture in the Last Decade* (Cambridge: Cambridge University Press, 1995), pp. 1–19.

Hadfield, Andrew, *Shakespeare and Renaissance Politics* (London: Bloomsbury Arden Shakespeare, 2004).

Hamilton, Donna, 'The State of Law in *Richard II*', *Shakespeare Quarterly* 34.1 (1983), pp. 5–17.

Harrawood, Michael, 'High-Stomached Lords: Imagination, Force, and the Body in Shakespeare's *Henry VI* Plays', *Journal for Early Modern Cultural Studies* 7.1 (2007), pp. 78–95.

Haverkamp, Anselm, '*Richard II*, Bracton, and the End of Political Theology', *Law and Literature* 16.3 (2004), pp. 313–26.

Hill, Geoffrey, *Broken Hierarchies: Poems 1952–2012*, ed. Kenneth Haynes (Oxford: Oxford University Press, 2013).

Hillman, David, and Carlo Mazzio, 'Introduction', in David Hillman and Carlo Mazzio (eds), *The Body in Parts: Fantasies of Corporeality in Early Modern Europe* (New York: Routledge, 1997), pp. xi–xxix.

Hobbes, Thomas, *Leviathan*, ed. C. B. McPherson (Harmondsworth: Penguin, 1968).

Höfele, Andreas, *Stage, Stake, and Scaffold: Humans and Animals in Shakespeare's Theatre* (Oxford: Oxford University Press, 2011).

Honigman, E. A. J., 'Introduction', *King John* (2nd Arden edn) (London: Methuen, 1954).

Howard, Jean E., and Phyllis Rackin, *Engendering a Nation: A Feminist Account of Shakespeare's English Histories* (London: Routledge, 1997).

Hunt, Maurice, 'The "Breaches" of Shakespeare's *The Life of King Henry the Fifth*', *College Literature* 41.4 (2014), pp. 7–24.

Hutson, Lorna, 'Not the King's Two Bodies: Reading the Body Politic in Shakespeare's *Henry IV* Plays', in Victoria Kahn and Lorna Hutson (eds), *Rhetoric and Law in Early Modern Europe* (New Haven: Yale University Press, 2001), pp. 166–89.

Jackson, Ken, '"Is It God or the Sovereign Exception?": Giorgio Agamben's *Homo Sacer* and Shakespeare's *King John*', *Literature and Religion* 38.3 (2006), pp. 85–100.

*John Stubbs's Gaping Gulf with Letters and Other Relevant Documents*, ed. Lloyd E. Berry (Charlottesville: University Press of Virginia, 1970).

Jorgensen, Paul A., 'The "Dastardly Treachery" of Prince John of Lancaster', *PMLA* 76.5 (1961), pp. 488–92.

Jowett, John, and Gary Taylor, 'The Three Texts of *2 Henry VI*', *Studies in Bibliography* 40 (1987), pp. 31–50.

Kahn, Victoria, *The Future of Illusion: Political Theology and Early Modern Texts* (Chicago: University of Chicago Press, 2014).

—, 'Political Theology and Fiction in *The King's Two Bodies*', *Representations* 106 (2009), pp. 77–101.

Kantorowicz, Ernst, *The King's Two Bodies* [1957] (Princeton: Princeton University Press, 1997).

Kendall, Gillian Murray, 'Overkill in Shakespeare', *Shakespeare Quarterly* 43.1 (1992), pp. 33–50.

Knapp, James A., 'Beyond Materiality in Shakespeare Studies', *Literature Compass* 11.10 (2014), pp. 677–90.

Knapp, Jeffrey, 'Preachers and Players in Shakespeare's England', *Representations* 44 (autumn 1993), pp. 29–59.

Knight, G. Wilson, *The Olive and the Sword: A Study of England's Shakespeare* (Oxford: Oxford University Press, 1944).

Lakoff, George, and Mark Johnson, *Metaphors We Live By* (Chicago: University of Chicago Press, 1980).

Lemon, Rebecca, 'Sacking Falstaff', in David B. Goldstein and Amy L. Tigner (eds), *Culinary Shakespeare: Staging Food and Drink in Early Modern England* (Pittsburgh: Duquesne University Press, 2016), pp. 113–32.

Levine, Nina, 'Extending Credit in the *Henry IV* Plays', *Shakespeare Quarterly* 51.4 (2000), pp. 403–31.

Lezra, Jacques, *Wild Materialism: The Ethic of Terror and the Modern Republic* (New York: Fordham University Press, 2010).
Lorenz, Philip, *The Tears of Sovereignty: Perspectives of Power in Renaissance Drama* (New York: Fordham University Press, 2013).
Miller, J. Hillis, 'Derrida Enisled', *Critical Inquiry* 33.2 (2007), pp. 248–76.
More, Thomas, *The History of King Richard III*, ed. George M. Logan (Indianapolis: Indiana University Press, 2005).
Nancy, Jean-Luc, *Being-Singular-Plural*, trans. Robert D. Richardson and Anne E. O'Byrne (Stanford: Stanford University Press, 2000).
Norbrook, David, 'The Emperor's New Body? *Richard II*, Ernst Kantorowicz, and the Politics of Shakespeare Criticism', *Textual Practice* 10 (1996), pp. 329–57.
Nowottny, Winifred, *The Language Poets Use* (London: The Athlone Press, 1962).
Olson, Greta, 'Richard III's Animalistic Criminal Body', *Philological Quarterly* 82.3 (2003), pp. 301–23.
Palfrey, Simon, *Shakespeare's Possible Worlds* (Cambridge: Cambridge University Press, 2014).
Parker, Patricia, *Literary Fat Ladies: Rhetoric, Gender, Property* (London: Methuen, 1987).
Paster, Gail, *Humoring the Body: Emotions and the Shakespearean Stage* (Chicago: University of Chicago Press, 2004).
Persons, Robert, *A Conference About the Next Succession to the Crown of England* (St Omer, 1594).
Puttenham, George, *The Arte of English Poesie* (London, 1589).
—, 'The Art of English Poesy', in *Sidney's The Defence of Poesy and Selected Renaissance Literary Criticism*, ed. Gavin Alexander (Harmondsworth: Penguin, 2004), pp. 55–204.
Pye, Christopher, *The Storm at Sea: Political Aesthetics in the Time of Shakespeare* (New York: Fordham University Press, 2015).
Rabkin, Norman, 'Rabbits, Ducks, and *Henry V*', *Shakespeare Quarterly* 28.3 (1977), pp. 279–96.
Rackin, Phyllis, *Stages of History: Shakespeare's English Chronicles* (Ithaca: Cornell University Press, 1990).
Rambuss, Richard, *Spenser's Secret Career* (Cambridge: Cambridge University Press, 1993).
Rousseau, Jean-Jacques, *The Social Contract*, trans. Maurice Cranston (Harmondsworth: Penguin, 1968).
Rowe, Katherine, *Dead Hands: Fictions of Agency: Renaissance to Modern* (Stanford: Stanford University Press, 2000).
Salmon, J. H. M., and Ralph E. Giesey, 'Introduction', in François Hotman, *Francogalia*, ed. Ralph E. Giesey, trans. J. H. M. Salmon (Cambridge: Cambridge University Press 1972).
Santner, Eric, *The Royal Remains: The People's Two Bodies and the Endgames of Sovereignty* (Chicago: University of Chicago Press, 2011).
Schmitt, Carl, *Political Theology: Four Chapters on the Concept of Sovereignty*, trans. George Schwah (Chicago: University of Chicago Press, 2005).
Schonhorn, Manuel, *Defoe's Politics: Parliament, Power, Kingship and Robinson Crusoe* (Cambridge: Cambridge University Press, 1991).

Schwyzer, Philip, *Shakespeare and the Remains of Richard III* (Oxford: Oxford University Press, 2013).
Shakespeare, William, *King Henry IV Part Two*, ed. James C. Bulman (London: Bloomsbury, 2016).
—, *The New Oxford Shakespeare* (Modern Critical Edition), ed. Gabriel Egan and Gary Taylor (Oxford: Oxford University Press, 2016).
—, *Richard II*, ed. Charles R. Forker (London: Cengage, 2002).
—, *Richard III* (3rd Arden edn), ed. James R. Siemon (London: Methuen, 2009).
Shannon, Laurie, *The Accommodated Animal: Cosmopolity in Shakespeare's Locales* (Chicago: University of Chicago Press, 2013).
—, *Sovereign Amity: Figures of Friendship in Shakespearean Contexts* (Chicago: University of Chicago Press, 2002).
Sharpe, J. A., *Judicial Punishment in England* (London: Faber and Faber, 1990).
Sherry, Richard, *A Treatise of Schemes and Tropes* (London, 1550).
Shuger, Deborah, *Political Theologies in Shakespeare's England: The Sacred and the State in* Measure for Measure (London: Palgrave, 2001).
Skinner, Quentin, *The Foundations of Modern Political Thought, Volume 1: The Renaissance* (Cambridge: Cambridge University Press, 1978).
—, *The Foundations of Modern Political Thought, Volume 2: The Age of Reformation* (Cambridge: Cambridge University Press, 1978).
Somerville, J. P., *Royalists and Patriots: Politics and Ideology in England 1603–1640* (London: Longman, 1999).
Taylor, Gary, and Rory Loughnane, 'The Canon and Chronology', in *The New Oxford Shakespeare* (Authorship Companion), ed. Gabriel Egan and Gary Taylor (Oxford: Oxford University Press, 2017), pp. 496–9.
Thomas, Keith, *Man and the Natural World: Changing Attitudes in England 1500–1800* (Harmondsworth: Penguin, 1983).
Tillyard, E. M. W., *Shakespeare's History Plays* (London: Chatto and Windus, 1959).
Traister, Barbara, 'The King's One Body: Unceremonial Kingship in *King John*', in Deborah Curren-Aquino (ed.), King John: *New Perspectives* (Newark: University of Delaware Press, 1989), pp. 91–8.
Turner, Henry S., *The Corporate Commonwealth: Pluralism and Political Factions in England 1516–1651* (Chicago: University of Chicago Press, 2016).
Vergil, Polydore, *Three Books of Polydore Vergil's English History*, ed. Sir Henry Ellis (London: Camden Society, 1844).
Watson, Robert, 'The Ecology of Self in *Midsummer Night's Dream*', in Lynne Bruckner and Dan Brayton (eds), *Ecocritical Shakespeare* (Burlington, VT: Ashgate, 2011), pp. 33–56.
Wills, David, *Prosthesis* (Stanford: Stanford University Press, 1995).
Wolin, Sheldon S., *Politics and Vision: Continuity and Innovation in Western Political Thought* (Princeton: Princeton University Press, 2016).
Yu, Jeffrey J., 'Shakespeare's *Julius Caesar*, Erasmus's *Copia*, and Sentential Ambiguity', *Comparative Drama* 41.1 (2007), pp. 79–106.
Zimmerman, Susan, *The Early Modern Corpse and Shakespeare's Theatre* (Edinburgh: Edinburgh University Press, 2005).

# Index

absolutism, 11, 22–3, 25, 39–40, 43, 53, 67, 77–9, 83, 95, 126, 136
Agamben, Giorgio, 16, 18–19, 26, 52, 66–7, 71, 96
Aristotle, 71

baroque, 1, 4–6, 11–12, 38
Benjamin, Walter, 4–6, 11, 25, 38
Berger Jr., Harry, 8–9, 46
Bodin, Jean, 13, 18, 22–3, 26, 28, 67, 75, 77, 78, 79–81, 82–3, 84–5, 96, 124, 138

capital punishment, 10, 61–7, 71, 91–2, 105–7, 130–1
Cicero, 76–7
Cooper, Farah Karim, 75
*copia*, 8, 101–5, 107–9, 113, 128

Defoe, Daniel, *Robinson Crusoe*, 39–43, 55n15
Deleuze, Gilles, 5, 12
deputisation, 67, 78, 81–3, 94–5, 110–11, 132–3, 138
Derrida, Jacques, 8, 26–7, 39–41, 46, 48–9, 51, 61–2, 66, 76, 84–6, 127, 129, 133

Elizabeth I, 21, 28, 38, 66, 91–2, 132, 135
Elyot, Thomas, 10–11, 12
Erasmus, Desiderius, 102, 104
Erne, Lukas, 8

Forsett, Edward, 13–16
Foucault, Michel, 11–13, 15

Gil, Daniel Juan, 18–19, 23, 96

hands, 20, 27, 37, 39, 53, 75, 76, 79, 81–2, 84–97, 127
Haverkamp, Anselm, 51–2
heads, 20, 38, 45, 62, 131–2
*hendiadys*, 7
heredity, 3, 78, 95
Hill, Geoffrey, 121, 139n10
Hobbes, Thomas, 13, 23, 31, 75–6, 78, 85, 96–7
Hotman, François, 23
Howard, Jean and Phyllis Rackin, 88, 131, 135
Hutson, Lorna, 51, 94–5

Jakobson, Roman, 78–9
Johnson, Mark and George Lakoff, 15

Kahn, Victoria, 25
Kantorowicz, Ernst, 46, 49–54, 86, 94, 96
knees, 3–4, 36–7, 38

Lezra, Jacques, 26, 85

metonymy *see* synecdoche
Miller, J. Hillis, 41, 46
Montaigne, Michel de, 36
More, Thomas, 121–2, 127, 128

Nancy, Jean Luc, 41
Nashe, Thomas, 29, 86
necks, 20, 61, 62, 68–72

Ovid, 37–8, 104, 134

Palfrey, Simon, 7–8
Paster, Gail Kern, 16–18
Persons, Robert, 23
Plowden, Edmund, 51

*poesis*, 3, 5–6, 20, 23, 24–5
pronouns, 47–9, 53, 63, 64, 109–10, 129–30
prosthesis, 72, 75, 76, 78, 79, 81, 84–7, 95
Puttenham, George, 76–7, 79, 82, 103–4
Pye, Christopher, 5–6

Rabkin, Norman, 59–60
resistance theory, 21, 23, 77, 82
Rousseau, Jean-Jacques, 39, 43, 55n10

Santner, Eric, 16, 71
Schmitt, Carl, 18–19, 25, 26, 51–2, 67, 126
Schwyzer, Philip, 122
Shakespeare, William
  *All is True*, 84
  *As You Like It*, 13, 127
  *Coriolanus*, 4
  *The First Part of the Contention*, 1–9
  *Henry IV* part one, 90, 101–19
  *Henry IV* part two, 94–5, 101–19, 124
  *Henry V*, 9–10, 12–13, 20, 44, 59–72, 124, 125
  *Henry VI* part one, 28–30, 86–7, 124
  *Henry VI* part three, 20, 35–6
  *Henry VI* part two, 1–9, 47
  *Julius Caesar*, 102–3
  *King John*, 20, 75–97, 131–2, 138
  *King Lear*, 68
  *Measure for Measure*, 50, 62
  *A Midsummer Night's Dream*, 37, 43, 68, 90, 127
  *Richard II*, 4, 25–6, 27, 35–54, 81–2, 94, 118, 124, 134
  *Richard III*, 91, 121–38
  *The Tempest*, 44
  *Titus Andronicus*, 98n14, 127
  *The Two Gentlemen of Verona*, 68
  *The Winter's Tale*, 37, 68, 133
Shannon, Laurie, 27–8, 35, 129, 134
Shuger, Deborah, 50–1
Smith, Thomas, 24
Stubbs, John, 98n14
synecdoche, 75–82, 86–7, 95
*synonimia*, 7

throats *see* necks
Turner, Henry, 24–5, 61

Vergil, Polydore, 121, 123–4
*Vindiciae Contra Tyrranos see* resistance theory
Virgil, 42

Wills, David, 75, 86

Zimmerman, Susan, 7, 11

EU representative:
Easy Access System Europe
Mustamäe tee 50, 10621 Tallinn, Estonia
Gpsr.requests@easproject.com

www.ingramcontent.com/pod-product-compliance
Lightning Source LLC
Chambersburg PA
CBHW070359240426
43671CB00013BA/2567